Project AIR FORCE

THE IMPLICATIONS OF THE POSSIBLE END OF THE ARAB-ISRAELI CONFLICT FOR GULF SECURITY

Zalmay M. Khalilzad
David A. Shlapak
Daniel L. Byman

Prepared for the
United States Air Force

RAND

The Arab-Israel peace process has made significant strides in recent years. Historically, the conflict between Arabs and the Jewish state has complicated U.S. dealings—including arms sales, military presence, and military operations—in the Middle East, particularly in the vital Gulf region. The conflict's possible end may offer the chance for the United States to improve its position in the region. The purpose of this report is to explore the implications of a possible end of the Arab-Israeli conflict for U.S. military—especially Air Force—operations in the Persian Gulf region. Such a study is necessary if the United States is to take advantage of the many and diverse benefits of peace, which will affect U.S. operations throughout the Middle East.

This study was conducted as part of the Strategy and Doctrine program of Project AIR FORCE, headed by Dr. Zalmay M. Khalilzad. The study was sponsored by the Director of Plans, Headquarters, U.S. Air Force (AF/XOX).

PROJECT AIR FORCE

Project AIR FORCE, a division of RAND, is the Air Force federally funded research and development center (FFRDC) for studies and analysis. It provides the Air Force with independent analyses of policy alternatives affecting the development, employment, combat readiness, and support of current and future aerospace forces. Research is being performed in three programs: Strategy and Doctrine, Force Modernization and Employment, and Resource Management and System Acquisition.

ASSUMPTIONS ABOUT AN ARAB-ISRAELI PEACE

Most of the research for this study was carried out during 1995, when the prospects for peace between Israel and its Arab neighbors seemed strong. The assassination of Prime Minister Yitzhak Rabin, the continuation of Palestinian terrorism, and the clashes between the Palestinian Authority and the new Israeli government of Benjamin Netanyahu all suggest that an immediate end to conflict is not likely. Nevertheless, because peace remains a possibility—even if it may take longer than hoped—it is important to understand fully the many security implications of a settlement.

Many of the benefits of peace for the U.S. military that are listed in this report may not be achieved until further progress toward a comprehensive settlement is made. For example, we note that as the Palestinian issue loses its appeal as a rallying cry in the Gulf, Israel will become a more legitimate state that is entitled to self-defense. Thus, were a Desert Storm–like crisis to arise, Israel could defend itself without splitting a U.S.–Arab coalition. If the peace process stalls and Israel remains a regional pariah, however, it is highly unlikely that the Gulf states will accept even a minimal security role for Israel in the region. Such a situation may require the United States again to devote considerable resources to defending Israel's security if a crisis arises.

Although some readers may consider a study assessing the benefits of peace to be premature, we believe it is important to begin thinking about such issues now. If the United States is to maximize the benefits of a peace agreement, it must begin understanding exactly how peace might improve its own position in the region. As this report makes clear, many of the benefits of peace require cooperation between Israel and the United States' Arab allies. Such cooperation is difficult and may take years to implement. We hope that this report will enable the U.S. military to begin implementation of the steps we recommend as peace progresses.

CONTENTS

FIGURES

TABLES

The security of the Persian Gulf remains a vital U.S. interest and, if anything, its relative importance has increased in recent years. In 1994, approximately 30 percent of U.S. oil imports came from Saudi Arabia alone. This figure appears likely to grow in the coming years. U.S. allies are even more dependent on Gulf oil, and the Gulf region contains roughly 60 percent of the world's proven oil reserves. Furthermore, the United States relies on the Gulf states to help resist the anti-Western regimes in Iran and Iraq. But the Gulf is not the only U.S. concern in the Middle East. Ensuring the security of Israel has been the other key U.S. interest in the region. Washington's ties to Israel, however, have been perceived as a sticking point in U.S.– Gulf ties, complicating U.S. policy in the region and the U.S. relationship with key Arab states.

The political landscape in the Middle East has changed dramatically in the past six years. The changes affect the nature of threats to U.S. interests in the region and how the United States might deal with them. The collapse of the Soviet Union has weakened the relative position of states allied with Moscow and has forced them to seek new sources of financial and military support, leading several to move closer to Washington and its moderate Arab allies. The U.S.– led military defeat of Iraq helped to redress the military balance in the Persian Gulf region, significantly reducing the near-term Iraqi military threat and providing an opportunity for an unprecedented coalition of Arab, Islamic, and Western nations to work together to roll back Iraqi aggression. The war against Iraq also strengthened U.S. ties to the Gulf states and enhanced the U.S. position as the leading extra-regional security partner. Finally, progress on peace between Israel and its Arab neighbors raises the prospect that many important aspects of this divisive and long-standing dispute will be settled.

Yet, despite these positive changes, the region remains unstable. The Gulf states face the prospect of internal unrest, with both economic and political reformers and Islamists criticizing area regimes. Iran and Iraq oppose U.S. influence in the region and seek to dominate their neighbors. Iran and Iraq themselves are unstable, and there is a significant possibility that internal crises may prompt the regimes in one or the other of these countries to attempt aggression against their neighbors.

Whether and how an Arab-Israeli peace will affect these sources of instability remain open questions. If the United States can leverage the benefits of peace, its ability to defend its interests in the Persian Gulf under a wide variety of conditions will be improved. Indeed, in some scenarios, Israel, the Middle East's leading military power, could also play a larger direct military role in Gulf affairs.

This report is intended to analyze the many implications of an Arab-Israeli peace for the security situation in the Persian Gulf, paying particular attention to the implications of that peace for U.S. Air Force operations. To this end, we describe the past effect of the Arab-Israeli crisis on the security environment in the Persian Gulf by noting the history of U.S.–Gulf state cooperation up to and including Operation Desert Storm. To assess the depth and range of that effect, we interviewed a wide range of U.S. and Middle Eastern officials and experts. We then discuss how peace might affect many of the problems that plagued U.S.–Gulf relations in the past. To illustrate our conclusions, we present a range of scenarios that would require U.S. military operations in the region. In these scenarios, we detail how peace might make such operations easier and what role, if any, Israeli forces might play.

U.S. TIES TO ISRAEL AND THEIR PAST EFFECT ON THE GULF

America's relations with Israel have long complicated U.S. ties to the Gulf states, particularly for military operations:

- Concerns over Israel's security led Washington to limit U.S. arms sales to the Gulf, hurting U.S. efforts to help the Gulf states defend themselves and prompting those states to turn elsewhere for supplies.

- U.S. ties to Israel made Gulf leaders more sensitive to and more wary about the possibility of having strong, open relations with Washington, complicating U.S. planning and prepositioning efforts in the region.

- After the 1973 War, U.S. support for Israel led the Gulf states to use their dominant position in the oil market to punish the United States and other oil consumers, leading to huge price increases and concomitant economic disruptions in the West.

- Partly because of the Gulf states' antipathy toward Israel, Israel was not included as part of the U.S. Central Command's (USCENTCOM's) Area of Responsibility (AOR), despite its location in the Middle East.

- During Desert Storm, the United States feared that Israeli participation would split the coalition. Consequently, the U.S.–led coalition devoted considerable resources to defending Israel against Iraqi missile attacks rather than letting Israel defend itself.

- Much of the influence of the Arab-Israeli dispute on Gulf security was indirect or implicit. U.S. officials believed that certain steps, such as creating a large-scale U.S. presence in the region to deter aggression, were not possible, because of Gulf state sensitivity, and learned simply not to bring them up during discussions with Gulf officials.

DESERT STORM: A TURNING POINT

During Operation Desert Storm, Arab sensitivity regarding U.S. ties to Israel raised the possibility that the coalition would fragment. When Iraq launched Scud missiles at Israel, many Arab leaders did not want Israel to retaliate for the Iraqi attacks for fear of angering Arab populations, and U.S. officials believed a direct Israeli role might split the anti-Iraq coalition. Therefore, the United States—to convince the Israelis that they did not need to take matters into their own hands—had to devote substantial resources to hunt and to defend against the missiles.

During Desert Storm, the United States built up political goodwill among its Arab allies, and U.S. military suppliers broadened their contacts in the Gulf—dramatically changing U.S. influence in and access to the Persian Gulf region. Following Desert Storm, the United States signed access agreements with Kuwait, Bahrain, Qatar, and the United Arab Emirate (UAE) and began prepositioning large amounts of military equipment in the region. U.S. military exercises with Gulf Cooperation Council (GCC) states have had a manifold increase since the end of the Gulf War.

CAUTIOUS PROGRESS ON COOPERATION

In the past six years, Israel and its Arab neighbors have made dramatic progress toward a comprehensive peace, but many problems remain unresolved. Since Desert Storm, Israel has signed a peace agreement with Jordan, made progress in negotiations with Syria and the Gulf states, provided the Palestinians with limited autonomy, and otherwise moved to defuse its long-standing conflict with the Arab world. Although this progress is remarkable, many contentious issues—including the fate of the Golan Heights, the status of Jerusalem, the rights of Palestinian returnees, and water rights—remain unresolved. The slow pace of negotiations, Palestinian terrorism, and the election of Benjamin Netanyahu in 1996 suggest that many Palestinians and Israelis are ambivalent about the peace negotiations and that further progress, if it occurs at all, may take years or decades.

In any event, the benefits of peace will be limited and slow to accrue. Gulf leaders and citizens—particularly Islamic militants—will remain suspicious of the United States and will not be eager to improve relations dramatically. Moreover, Israelis and most Gulf residents are suspicious of each other, and neither side sees an immediate need for joint security cooperation. The Camp David Accords should be a caution to optimists: Fifteen years after the signing of peace, relations between Egypt and Israel remain lukewarm, and large parts of the Egyptian populace are still hostile to Israel.

But the problems of the present should not obscure the progress made so far and the potential for future cooperation. Many of those who rallied against an Israeli role—Palestinians, Arab nationalists, such hard-line states as Syria and Iraq, and communist countries—now are reduced in power or no longer oppose Israel. Furthermore, incentives for cooperation between Israel and the Gulf states are many. Israel and the Gulf share common adversaries such as Iraq and Iran. In addition, the changing means of war, particularly the spread of ballistic missiles and Iranian-backed terrorism, imply that Israel's security no longer is ensured simply by having peace with its immediate neighbors.

Much could be done if Israel and the Gulf states worked together. Low-level intelligence cooperation against these potential foes is likely to be a first step toward security cooperation and may begin in the near term. Other areas of potential cooperation in the short-term include measures to fight terrorism and strengthen friendly governments. The long-term benefits could be even greater: Israel is the region's leading military power, and its capabilities could affect any military conflict in the Middle East.

Peace has already led to limited cooperation between Israel and several Gulf states. Qatar and Oman have moved to consolidate their relationship with Israel, engaging in talks that include joint commercial ventures. Security cooperation, however, is a long way off. Saudi Arabia, the key state in the region, has moved slowly and is likely to keep Israel at arm's length for the foreseeable future.

SCENARIOS FOR POSSIBLE ISRAELI CONTRIBUTIONS

This report focuses on an optimistic vision of continued progress on peace between Israel and its neighbors. To illustrate how an Arab-Israeli peace will affect U.S. military operations in the Gulf region if a crisis does occur, we have developed several scenarios that are plausible in the coming years: enforcing a "red line" inside Iraq; defending Kuwait and Saudi Arabia against Iraq; defending Saudi Arabia against a coordinated Iraqi-Yemeni attack; defending against an Iraqi-Yemeni attack and Iranian opportunism; defending the peninsula littoral against Iran; helping the Al Saud cope with internal instability; and deterring Iran in the event of an Iraqi collapse. The scenarios are intended to improve U.S. thinking on how to receive the full benefits of a peace rather than to predict the most likely course of events in the region. They suggest that the resolution of the Arab-Israeli dispute, which allows open Israeli cooperation with the United States and tacit Israeli cooperation with the Gulf states, will improve the United States' ability to defend the region in a crisis. Israeli participation, however, will be more significant in some crises than in others.

IMPLICATIONS FOR THE UNITED STATES

If the peace process continues to improve relations between Israel and its neighbors, it will improve the U.S. political and strategic position in the Gulf region:

- Although many Gulf residents will remain opposed to a U.S. presence in the region for religious or Arab nationalist reasons, anti–United States hostility stemming from U.S. support of Israel will lessen, enhancing the U.S. image in the region.

- As relations between the Arab world and Israel improve, the Gulf states will be less likely to use their oil assets to press the United States to cut its support for Israel.

- U.S. arms sales to the region, while still likely to receive Israeli scrutiny, will probably become less politically sensitive in the United States.

- If a major regional crisis similar to the Iraqi invasion of Kuwait were to occur again, Israel would no longer prove a heavy burden to the U.S. military. If Israel were attacked, it could defend itself and retaliate without shattering a coalition.

- In the event of a crisis in the Gulf, Israel's own military and logistics assets might prove helpful to deploying U.S. forces or, *in extremis*, to the Gulf states themselves. Such assistance would be particularly useful if internal instability or military vulnerability limited U.S. basing on the peninsula or elsewhere in the region.

- An Arab-Israeli peace also should aid U.S. Air Force operations in the region if a crisis occurred. Access to Israeli airspace—or Israeli-Jordanian airspace—for overflight for operations in the Gulf would be particularly important should routes through Egypt be unavailable. Israel also offers a site for *additional* prepositioning and basing for Gulf contingencies. Prepositioning and basing in Israel will be of only marginal value to operations in the Gulf region if facilities and equipment in Saudi Arabia are available. However, should access to the Kingdom be restricted, equipment and bases in Israel would become more important.

The United States should consider taking several steps to improve the chances for an Israeli contribution to Gulf security. First, the United States should encourage Gulf-Israeli cooperation. A quiet dialogue between Israel and the Gulf states on issues of common concern, particularly Iraq and Iran, might be a good starting point. This limited dialogue could be complemented by a broader regional dialogue on the security of the region that included the GCC states, Israel, Egypt, Jordan, and Turkey. Second, the U.S. military—especially the Air Force—should begin considering additional options that the peace process provides for projecting power to this region— options that include contributions from Israel alone or in combination with others such as the Jordanians and Turks. Third, the United States should consider developing a plan for facilitating cooperation among the military forces—especially air forces—of the United States, GCC, Israel, Turkey, Egypt, and Jordan, with a focus on Gulf security.

These steps should encourage habits of cooperation and teach the parties to consider the assets and needs of the other during exercises and other forms of military-to-military cooperation. Finally, changing the AOR of USCENTCOM to include Israel and the remaining Arab states and perhaps "dual-hatting" Turkey—arranging for both CENTCOM and the European Command (EUCOM) to have authority there—might improve the U.S. military's ability to integrate its regional security policy into a greater whole and facilitate broader regional military cooperation focused on threats to the Gulf.

ACKNOWLEDGMENTS

The authors would like to thank the following individuals for their input into this project: Zbigniew Brzezinski, Frank Carlucci, Walter Cutler, Margaret Dean, Major David Frazee, Major Phillip Gibbons, Richard Haass, Art Hughes, Paul Jourdeini, General John Jumper (USAF), Geoffrey Kemp, Ellen Laipson, David Levi, the late Major General Robert Linhard, Robert McFarlane, Sam Lewis, Bruce Pease, Bruce Riedel, Alina Romanowski, Mohammed al Sabah, James Schlesinger, Fred Smith, David Welch, and Paul Wolfowitz, as well as others both in the United States and abroad who cannot be mentioned. This thanks does not imply that they agree with us on all aspects of our assessments and our recommendations.

We would also like to thank our RAND colleagues, Joseph Kechichian, John Bordeaux, Paul Davis, Laura Morrison, Walter Nelson, David Ochmanek, Deborah Peetz, Luetta Pope, and David Thaler, for their assistance.

Chapter One

INTRODUCTION

The past six years have witnessed dramatic changes in the Middle East and, indeed, throughout the entire world. The collapse of the Soviet Union and the discrediting of communism permanently altered the face of the Middle East and jarred long-standing alliances. States and movements friendly to Moscow, such as the Palestine Liberation Organization (PLO) and Syria, have had to look elsewhere for financial, military, and diplomatic support, leading them to reduce their opposition to U.S. goals in the region. South Yemen, another Soviet client, collapsed entirely as a viable entity, leading to its merger—sustained by force—with North Yemen. These developments, and the decrease in Moscow's influence in general, have led to more freedom of action in the region for the United States.

The Iraqi invasion of Kuwait, and the subsequent U.S.–led liberation of the sheikhdom, also had dramatic effects on the region. The defeat of Iraq substantially reduced the Iraqi military threat to the Persian Gulf. Moreover, it removed a growing military threat to Israel and prevented the emergence of another nuclear power in the region. The invasion also fostered a coalition among a new bloc of Arab states—led by Saudi Arabia, Syria, and Egypt—to resist Iraqi aggression. Finally, U.S. military might and resolve were convincingly demonstrated, reinforcing the U.S. position as the predominant outside state in the region and leading to an increased U.S. presence in the region.

The end of the Cold War and the change in alignments resulting from Desert Storm facilitated diplomatic breakthroughs that are progressing toward an Arab-Israeli peace. And with that end, both Syria and the Palestinians suddenly found themselves short of financial backers and in need of improving ties to the West and to their moderate Arab allies. For the PLO, this support was desperately needed as rivals in the West Bank and Gaza, particularly the Islamic group HAMAS, began to gain support at the PLO's expense. The Palestinians' support for Iraq had angered the Gulf regimes—a leading source of jobs and financial support for the Palestinian cause—forcing the Palestinians to court the West and its allies once Iraq was defeated. Abandoned by Moscow, Syria was forced to give up any dream of achieving military parity with Israel, and needed hard currency to maintain its military and economy.

Progress in the Arab-Israeli peace process has come at a time when the stability of the Gulf region is under threat. Both Iran and Iraq harbor ambitions to be the region's hegemon and have, in the past, sought to change governments and borders in the region. Iran is building up its military and has already developed chemical (and probably biological) warfare capabilities. Tehran also is pursuing nuclear weapons capabilities. Iraq, which had extensive chemical and biological warfare stockpiles before Desert Storm and was close to building a nuclear weapon, would follow the same course were it not for U.N. sanctions. Should sanctions end, Iraq probably could quickly rebuild its chemical and biological stockpiles and might again seek to develop nuclear weapons. Iran is importing missiles from North Korea and China, and both Iran and Iraq have indigenous missile-development programs. By themselves, the Gulf Cooperation Council (GCC) states cannot yet meet these challenges. Cooperation among the GCC states remains limited by rivalries and suspicions that Saudi Arabia seeks to dominate the peninsula.

Internal problems compound the potential damage that Iran or Iraq could do. Several Gulf royal families are likely to face challenges to their rule from domestic opposition in the coming years. Potential sources of opposition include Islamists, liberals, and even rival ruling-family members. Compounding these problems are economic stagnation and a burgeoning population in a number of GCC states. Iran and Iraq could well attempt to take advantage of any internal problems within the Gulf states. (For a discussion of potential future fault lines in the Middle East, see Appendix A.)

Peace between Israel and its neighbors would open up a new chapter in Middle East history. Although neither Israel nor the Arab states will be quick to embrace each other, over time they may move closer as the importance of the Arab-Israeli conflict in the region diminishes and other security issues become more important. Israel shares concerns with the Gulf states for the threat posed by Iran and Iraq. To counter the various common threats, the United States, which has a stake in the security of both Israel and the Gulf states, can and should encourage and facilitate cooperation.

At issue are the two major U.S. security concerns in the Middle East: the security of Israel and that of the Persian Gulf. Political necessity has caused the U.S. military to treat these issues as separate matters, despite the fact that the security challenges of these two regions have often been intertwined. A resolution of the Arab-Israeli conflict offers an opportunity for the United States to treat the Middle East as a whole in ways that can protect U.S. interests in both the Gulf and the Levant.

This study is intended to help the U.S. military—particularly the U.S. Air Force (USAF)—capitalize on positive changes in the Middle East security environment that may come about after a comprehensive Arab-Israeli peace. To this end, we offer an overview of the importance of the Persian Gulf and how the Arab-Israeli dispute has complicated U.S. efforts to defend this critical region. We pay particular attention to U.S. problems during Operation Desert Storm. We then discuss the current status of the Arab-Israeli peace settlement and assess the likelihood of both Israel and the Gulf states agreeing to work together in the region. The study then details ways in which Israeli participation might aid the U.S. Air Force in future crises if peace reduces the stigma attached to an Israeli security role in the region. To illustrate the value of an Israeli role (and to demonstrate its limits), we describe seven scenarios in the Persian Gulf and assess how an Arab-Israeli peace might affect military operations. We conclude by noting the implications of the above points for the U.S. military and for the U.S. Air Force in particular.

The study also offers three appendices—one discussing future fault lines in the Middle East, a second on the state of U.S.–Israel cooperation today, and a third on the influence of weapons of mass destruction on Persian Gulf military operations—that are intended to help readers think about future problems facing the Middle East that may have a bearing on the conclusions of this study.

Chapter Two

THE IMPORTANCE OF THE PERSIAN GULF

To understand why implications of an Arab-Israeli peace for Gulf security should matter to the U.S. military and U.S. policymakers, we must first assess the importance of the Persian Gulf to the United States. This chapter describes how U.S. relations with the Gulf states have evolved and notes why the Gulf remains a vital U.S. interest today.

FROM WORLD WAR II TO DESERT STORM

The United States security presence in the Gulf goes back to World War II. In 1943, President Franklin D. Roosevelt declared the defense of Saudi Arabia vital to the defense of the United States (Stork and Wenger, 1991). At that time, Washington created the Persian Gulf Command to manage growing problems in Iran and other regions posing threats. In the same year, King `Abd al-Aziz secretly granted the United States the right to build a military airfield in Dhahran, which became an important U.S. base against the Axis. Also in 1943, the first U.S. advisory mission began working with Saudi forces. During World War II, the United States started maintaining a Naval presence in the Persian Gulf region.

Cooperation between the United States and the Gulf states increased after World War II as the United States implemented its policy of containment of Soviet expansionism. In 1949, Washington homeported the then-new Middle East Force on the British naval base at Bahrain; it remains stationed there to this day. By 1951, U.S. advisers were working with the Saudis on force plans and the development of a modern military infrastructure. In June of that year, Washington and Riyadh signed their first formal defense agreement, which established a permanent U.S. military mission in Saudi Arabia and gave the United States the use of Dhahran Airfield as a strategic air base (Cordesman, 1984).

The training of military forces and construction of military-related facilities were an important part of U.S. security assistance to the region. The United States provided schooling for officers and enlisted personnel through the grant Military Assistance Program, the Foreign Military Sales (FMS) system, and the grant-aid International Military Education and Training (IMET) program. Many regional air forces have received some USAF training, and Saudi ground forces have been given extensive training by American military personnel (U.S. Department of Defense, 1992). The U.S. Army Corps of Engineers also built most of Saudi Arabia's military infrastructure.

The Gulf was a key part of the U.S. effort to contain the Soviet Union in the 1950s. Located at the right flank of NATO and south of the Soviet heartland, the Gulf states provided staging areas from which strategic air forces could deter the Soviets, and where intelligence facilities could monitor Soviet buildups and U.S. Naval forces could be based. In 1955, two Gulf nations bordering the Soviet Union— Iraq and Iran—joined the U.S.–sponsored Baghdad Pact, an alliance intended to increase cooperation against the Soviet Union in the region. The alliance collapsed after the 1958 Iraqi revolution. The United States was willing to turn its facilities in Dhahran over to Saudi control in the early 1960s, because advances in aircraft and missile technology had reduced the need for some air bases overseas.

The Gulf states also played a role in countering Soviet opportunism in the Middle East. After Britain completed withdrawal from the Persian Gulf in 1971, President Richard Nixon announced that Saudi Arabia and Iran would be the "twin pillars" upon which the United States would depend in its effort to contain Moscow in the region. Although the Shah's Iran initially played the leading role, Saudi Arabia's importance increased tremendously after the Iranian revolution in 1978–1979. The United States also signed an access agreement with Oman in 1980, which gave the U.S. military access to Omani port and air facilities. In general, the Gulf states acted as a force for moderation in the turbulent Middle East. They were fiercely anti-communist and contributed money to anti-communist insurgencies and causes. Moreover, they tacitly opposed radical forms of Arab nationalism, which often had a strong anti-Western bent.

Compounding U.S. concerns for Soviet geostrategic aspirations in the Gulf was the region's importance to the U.S. economy and that of U.S. allies. Disruptions in the region's oil supply in the 1970s led to severe economic problems in the United States, Western Europe, and Japan. Following the embargo and production cutback imposed by the Organization of Petroleum Exporting Countries (OPEC) after the 1973 War, oil prices skyrocketed, causing the U.S. gross national product (GNP) to drop. When Iranian oil exports were stopped for several months following the Iranian revolution of 1979, the U.S. GNP again fell. Both oil shocks also increased inflation and led to a significant decrease in real wages (Rowen, 1988; Pindyck and Rotemberg, 1984).

The growth in U.S. and Western oil consumption, the increasing radicalism of Iran and Iraq, and the Gulf's proximity to the Soviet Union caused increased attention to be focused on the Gulf's security needs, particularly after the fall of the Shah in 1979. Following the Soviet invasion of Afghanistan, U.S. military planning began focusing on deterring a Soviet invasion of the region. In January 1980, President Jimmy Carter formally elevated the Persian Gulf to a "region of vital importance," declaring that "any attempt by an outside force to gain control of the Persian Gulf oil will be regarded as an assault on vital interests of the United States of America, and such an assault will be repelled by any means necessary, including military force" (Carter, 1980).

President Carter initiated the creation of the Rapid Deployment Joint Task Force, the forerunner of the U.S. Central Command (USCENTCOM), to enable the United States to deploy quickly an effective military force to the region. U.S. military planning to protect the Gulf focused on deterring a Soviet invasion by developing forces, plans, and regional arrangements that could allow the U.S. military promptly to respond to such an invasion or threat of invasion (Ross, 1981; McNaugher, 1985). In the event of Soviet aggression, U.S. strategy called for a forward defense of the region in the Zagros Mountains of Iran.

Western dependence on Gulf oil decreased in the 1980s, as the huge increases in oil prices in the 1970s caused consumption of and demand for oil to decline. Government-incentive programs in the West also increased conservation, further lowering demand. The rise in the price of oil also stimulated oil production in non-Gulf regions, where the high cost of production had previously limited output. By 1985, the Gulf provided only 20 percent of the noncommunist world's oil supplies, roughly half of what it provided in 1973.

THE IMPORTANCE OF THE GULF TODAY

The Persian Gulf has become more important to U.S. security concerns since the end of the Cold War. In the past, preparing for a war in Europe dominated U.S. security concerns. Today, in a shift that began under President George Bush's administration and is being continued by President Bill Clinton's administration, the United States is focusing on regional fronts, particularly in the Gulf and the Korean peninsula. The United States has increased its military presence in the Gulf in the past six years. Moreover, the region is likely to dominate the world supply of oil for the foreseeable future. As a percentage of total usage, the excess production capacity of non-Gulf producers has fallen since 1985, increasing the market power of the Gulf suppliers and the concentration of world production in the Gulf region.

Gulf Oil

The importance of Gulf oil is again increasing, both to the world and to the U.S. economy. The Gulf region contains 60 percent of the world's proven reserves of crude oil. Although the United States reduced its imports of Gulf oil following the price shocks of the 1970s, since 1985 the United States has imported a greater share of oil from the Gulf, rising from 20 percent of total consumption in 1985 to 33 percent in 1994. The Gulf's lower production costs and greater production capacity—both of which are more important as oil prices fall—have led Western consumers to again turn to the Gulf. If Iraq reentered the market or if the states of the former Soviet Union increased their oil exports, prices would fall even further, increasing the Gulf's competitive advantage. Both Iran and Iraq seek higher oil prices. Without a U.S. regional presence, they might threaten the Gulf states militarily to achieve this goal.

Saudi Arabian oil is particularly important. As of late 1994, the Kingdom controlled the largest known oil reserves in the world, conservatively estimated at 260 billion barrels, or about 27 percent of world reserves. Moreover, U.S. imports of crude oil and refined products were at an all-time high and growing. The American Petroleum Institute pegged oil imports at a record 10,059,000 barrels per day (b/d) for July 1994. The previous record was just less than 10 million b/d in early 1977, although total U.S. oil consumption was about 1 million b/d less at that time. Of the imports, which accounted for 58 percent of domestic demand in July 1994, 30 percent came from Saudi Arabia alone.

Hostile control over the Gulf oil reserves could spell disaster for the United States. Although a skeptic might claim that even a hostile power still must sell the oil, hostile states have, in the past, ignored economic self-interest to punish their enemies. Moreover, a supplier might refuse to sell oil at crucial moments, such as when the United States became involved in a war. Although the price of oil today is low and reserve levels appear to be increasing, the huge growth in oil consumption (particularly in East Asia) makes it likely that the market again will tighten in future years.

Stability and Security

In addition to oil, countries and individuals in the Gulf region can affect the stability and security of the United States and its allies. Iran and Iraq, both of which appear eager to gain nuclear weapons and ballistic missiles, reject the U.S. presence in the region, and remain hostile to pro-Western regional governments. Iran has led the rejectionist camp in opposing an Arab-Israeli peace and is the world's leading state sponsor of terrorism, supporting groups such as Hezbollah, the Palestinian Islamic Jihad, and organizations in Sudan, Algeria, and Afghanistan.

The Gulf states will continue to rely on the United States to ensure their security. Peninsula Shield, the Gulf Cooperation Council security force, is not yet strong enough to deal with the range of potential threats posed by Iran and Iraq. Its postwar efforts to work with Egypt and Syria foundered on both the cost of the troops and the Gulf states' perceptions about its unreliability. As a result, all the states of the Gulf have either continued or stepped up cooperation with the United States to ensure their security.[1]

---

[1]Nor are the GCC states free from conflicts among themselves. Several of these states, particularly Oman and Qatar, fear potential Saudi hegemony. To balance Saudi power, Muscat has sought good relations with Iran, Yemen, and, now, Israel. Doha, for its part, has clashed with the Saudis over border demarcation (in 1992) and maintains cordial relations with Iran and Iraq. Bahrain and Qatar have long quarreled over the ownership of the Hawar Islands, and this dispute has disrupted GCC cooperation, even during times of crisis such as the Gulf War. In the United Arab Emirates (UAE), several border disputes remain unresolved, including some that involve Oman.

Chapter Three

ISRAEL'S INFLUENCE ON THE U.S. PRESENCE IN THE GULF

The Arab-Israeli dispute and the Palestinian issue have complicated U.S. relations with the states of the Persian Gulf and have hindered U.S. efforts to provide for Gulf security. Although it is hard to separate rhetoric from reality on the Arab-Israeli conflict, the Arab-Israeli dispute has been an unwelcome distraction for U.S. officials, affecting Washington's ability to resist Soviet encroachment in the region and to maintain a steady supply of oil. During Operation Desert Storm, the Arab-Israeli dispute complicated U.S. military operations and threatened to split the coalition.

This chapter first notes the domestic pressures that compelled the Gulf governments to publicly distance themselves from Washington. It then discusses how this distancing and the dispute in general has affected U.S. interests in the region. Following this general discussion, we note how the dispute complicated Gulf security and U.S. military operations in the region before, during, and after Operation Desert Storm. Particular attention is paid to the difficulties faced by the U.S. Air Force.

DOMESTIC PRESSURES ON THE GULF STATES

Domestic pressure generated by the Arab-Israeli dispute has been one factor behind the Gulf states' resistance to a U.S. military presence on their soil. Giving bases to Israel's chief ally raised the domestic political costs of stationing U.S. forces in the region or even of maintaining close and open political and military ties to Washington. Domestic pressure stemmed from ordinary citizens, Arab nationalists, Islamic militants, expatriate workers, and regional rivals. When combined with the Gulf leaders' own antipathy toward Israel, this pressure led to hostility toward Israel in general and disputes with its chief backer, the United States.

The traditional rulers of the Gulf knew that the presence of foreign forces had long been a rallying cry in Middle Eastern revolutions and coups. In Iran and Libya, the presence of U.S. forces became a focus of revolutionary criticism before traditional leaders there were over-thrown. Critics of the regimes in Bahrain and Saudi Arabia fre-quently complained about existing, low-profile cooperation with the United States and cited U.S. support for Israel as proof of Washington's hostile intentions in the region. For example, in 1961 Prince Talal ibn `Abd al-Aziz—a "Free Prince" critic of the regime living in Cairo—called for King Saud to end the Dhahran Airfield use agreement (Quandt, 1981b).

Gulf leaders' personal security worries also led them to support the Palestinian cause and to maintain their distance from Washington. Gulf leaders feared Palestinian reprisals—whether in the form of criticism or assassination—against those who deviated from a hard line against Israel (Newsom, 1981). Gulf leaders also feared pressure from Damascus, which claimed to champion the Palestinian issue. Some may have even feared that they might be the target of Syrian-sponsored assassination attempts.

The populace in the Gulf may be even more hostile toward Israel than the ruling elites. Most Gulf residents under the age of 35—approximately 70 percent of the native population—grew up in a political atmosphere where the Palestinian issue was the *sine qua non* of Arab consciousness. Particularly after the 1967 War, Palestinian politics permeated the Arab media, educational insti-tutions, and youth movements. To demonstrate their commitment to Arab issues and to quiet critics, area regimes trumpeted their support for the Palestinians (Cordesman, 1984).

Arab Nationalism

In the 1950s and 1960s, the greatest pressure militating against close ties to the United States came from Arab nationalists. Dismayed by the growing domestic support for Arab nationalism as championed by Egyptian President Gamal Nasser, the House of Saud played down its ties to the United States. The `Al Saud's fears that Arab nationalists might lead to their downfall were not idle. During the 1950s and 1960s, Egypt, Iraq, Libya, and Yemen all saw traditional leaders replaced by Arab nationalists. At the same time, radical nationalists increasingly penetrated the Saudi military, and they were not satisfied with token efforts of the regime to distance itself from Washington (Cordesman, 1984).[1] Similarly, nationalists in Bahrain and Kuwait called for curtailing ties to the United States, citing Washington's support for Israel.

Islamic Radicalism

Although Arab nationalism has waned as a political force in the Gulf in recent years, particularly after the Iraqi invasion of Kuwait, Islamic radicalism has waxed, sustaining pressure on Gulf regimes to cut or curtail ties to Washington. The November 1979 uprising in Mecca, which was led by conservative religious and tribal figures, is only the most prominent instance of the threat religious militants pose to the House of Saud (Cordesman, 1984). Even pro-regime religious leaders such as Sheikh `Abd al-Aziz bin Baz called upon the government to avoid involvement in non-Islamic pacts and treaties, which presumably included formal defense ties to Washington (Kechichian, 1993). Part of the Saudi regime's legitimacy derives from its custodianship of the Muslim holy sites of Mecca and Medina. Given intense criticism on Islamic grounds by the clerical regime in Iran, Riyadh could not open itself to attacks on its religious bona fides by being soft on the Arab-Israeli dispute (Cordesman, 1984). In Bahrain and Kuwait, terrorism and protests by Islamic groups during the 1980s made the ruling families there cautious in their relations with Washington. Islamic militancy had an anti-Western tone, in part because of the unresolved Arab-Israeli dispute and the U.S. sponsorship of the Camp David process (Yorke, 1980).

Radical Arab and Muslim powers played on popular concerns about Israel to promote anti-American agendas. In the past, the presence of the U.S. Air Force at Dhahran Airfield had exposed the Saudis to

---

[1] Saudi Arabia hoped to win their support by gestures such as expelling the U.S. Point Four economic aid mission in 1954.

the charge of cooperating with Israel (Quandt, 1981b). Egyptian President Nasser pressed the Saudis not to join the Baghdad Pact or other U.S.–sponsored regional initiatives on the grounds that such a move would help Israel (Cordesman, 1984). After the United States deployed the Advanced Warning and Control System (AWACS) to the Gulf during the early days of the Iran-Iraq War, Libya broke off relations with the Kingdom, and Syria reacted by signing a Friendship and Cooperation Treaty with the Soviet Union (Kupchan, 1987). Iran and Iraq continue such pressure today and call for the Gulf states to cut ties to the United States.

Foreign workers in the Gulf states increased Gulf leaders' sensitivity to ties to the United States. Saudi Arabia's rulers feared that Palestinians might engage in terrorism out of frustration if no progress were made on a Palestinian homeland (Yorke, 1980). Kuwaitis in particular felt vulnerable on Palestinian issues as a result of their (pre–Gulf War) dependence on roughly 300,000 Palestinian expatriates. Although there were fewer Palestinians in Saudi Arabia, both Saudi Arabia and Kuwait felt exposed, since the Palestinians often enjoyed high-ranking government and commercial positions (Sterner, 1985). Thus, Kuwait supported many radical causes and avoided commitments to the United States that might have angered the Palestinian leadership (Cordesman, 1984; Amos and Magnus, 1985; and an interview with an expert who prefers to remain anonymous).

Such domestic pressures led Saudi Arabia to publicly promote the Palestinian cause even as the Kingdom moved closer to Washington. Riyadh was attempting to balance domestic political opinion, which was often hostile to the positions of the U.S. government, with its need for a security partner; the result was hostile, mainly anti-Israel, rhetoric tempered by tacit cooperation with the United States. Saudi leaders repeatedly stressed that they would not abandon the Palestinians in exchange for U.S. arms. As Islamist pressure increased, Saudi Arabia played up its demand for Arab and Muslim control of Jerusalem. For example, at the Islamic Conference in Taif, Saudi Arabia, in 1981, Riyadh tried to emphasize the issues of Jerusalem and Palestine in order to protect its Islamic bona fides (Binder, 1982).

Domestic pressures also have caused Gulf and Muslim leaders to ignore otherwise-sound strategic alliances. For example, in 1982 in private meetings with senior U.S. officials, King Fahd, Pakistan President Mohammad Zia, and Egyptian President Anwar Sadat recognized that an alliance that included them, the United States, and Israel against the Soviets would be logical. However, it was impossible to admit such strategic interests publicly, which prevented the implementation of such a strategically sound alliance (expert interview).

The degree of sensitivity to closer relations with the United States differed considerably among the Gulf states. Oman was more willing to work openly with the United States than were the other GCC states, whereas Kuwait was particularly critical of U.S. support for Israel. Saudi Arabia maintained close ties to Washington, but tried to play down those ties in public.

INFLUENCE OF THE DISPUTE ON THE UNITED STATES

The effect of the Arab-Israeli dispute and the Palestinian issue on Gulf–U.S. relations during the Cold War was not restricted to the Gulf states' hesitation to embrace the United States. The Arab-Israeli conflict sparked an oil-production cutback that triggered high levels of inflation, economic stagnation, and recession in the United States, and the dispute limited the United States' ability to make solid commitments to the Gulf region, particularly in arms sales.

The most serious effect of the Arab-Israeli dispute from the U.S. point of view—the 1973 oil embargo—followed the U.S. resupply of Israel in its war with Egypt and Syria. After the 1967 War, Riyadh made a half-hearted attempt to stop petroleum sales to Israel's Western supporters, but this stoppage failed because of the existing surplus capacity in the West. By 1973, however, consumption increases in the West left the United States and its allies dependent on the Gulf and other Arab states for oil. Thus, when the OPEC nations cut back production to bolster the oil embargo against Israel's supporters, prices soared, leading to economic problems in the West. The oil embargo also led Western European governments to break ranks with the United States in its support for Israel (Safran, 1978).

Israel also resisted U.S. efforts to bolster the militaries of the Gulf states. To ensure its own security, Israel sought to limit U.S. arms sales to the region in order to maintain a qualitative edge in equipment over potential Arab adversaries and also sought to keep Saudi Arabia's force-projection capabilities limited. Although Israeli opposition to the 1981 AWACS sale to Saudi Arabia has received the most coverage, Israeli opposition to arms sales to the Gulf states has existed since Israel's founding.

In 1955, only a few years after the first U.S. advisory mission began to help Saudi Arabia plan for its security, supporters of Israel in the United States tried to block the sale of the first 18 tanks to Saudi Arabia, resulting in a temporary halt of the sale. In time, both the Gulf states and the United States learned to choose arms with an eye toward Israel's domestic supporters as well as to Gulf security. For example, when the Saudis initially bought the F-15, they accepted that it would come with only three rather than five hard points, which limited its capability to be converted to attack missions. They also agreed not to purchase fuel-tank ("FAST") kits that would extend the planes' range. Later, in late 1985, the Saudis requested an F-15 upgrade package that would have created larger interoperable stocks and better facilities, but the administration's fear of losing midterm Senate elections caused it to vacillate, leading Riyadh eventually to purchase British-made Tornados (Cordesman, 1984, 1988).

By the mid-1980s, lobbying on behalf of Israel had virtually paralyzed the Reagan administration's effort to modernize even the smaller GCC states' forces. The result was that Gulf states such as Qatar and the UAE turned to Britain and France for weapons. Even during the 1988 reflagging effort—Operation Earnest Will—the Reagan administration could not win congressional approval for the sale of Stinger missiles to Bahrain (Cordesman, 1988).

The Egyptian-Israeli peace temporarily hurt the United States' diplomatic influence, as well. Camp David led Washington's two greatest Arab friends—Saudi Arabia and Egypt—to become antagonistic toward each other. Furthermore, as a result of Camp David, the great majority of Arab states, including Saudi Arabia and Jordan, broke off diplomatic relations with Egypt.

EFFECT OF DISPUTE ON GULF SECURITY BEFORE
OPERATION DESERT STORM

Although the United States has had a military presence in the Gulf for over 50 years, U.S. sensitivity to Israel's needs and Gulf states' concerns about domestic unrest hindered U.S. involvement in Gulf security. These difficulties manifested themselves in Gulf ambivalence toward an American presence, complications for U.S. planners, a lack of confidence in the United States' commitment to the region, interoperability and prepositioning problems, and political openings for U.S. rivals in the region.

Saudi Arabia and the smaller Gulf states were often ambivalent about the U.S. presence, in part as a result of U.S. support for Israel. As one European diplomat described the Saudi attitude toward a U.S. security role in the Gulf, "the United States should go away a little closer" (as quoted in Kheli and Staudenmaier, 1982). This ambivalence led to an "over-the-horizon" approach to security, whereby the U.S. presence on the ground was minimal while plans were made for a large U.S. deployment in the event of a crisis. This approach relied heavily on the U.S. Air Force, both in requiring a substantial U.S. capability to deploy quickly to the region and in acting as an early line of defense against possible Iraqi incursions into Saudi Arabia. Although Saudi Arabia officially rejected all superpower forces in the region, in reality it accepted the desirability of an offshore U.S. Naval presence in the Gulf, a U.S. presence in Oman and the horn of Africa, help from the United States to develop its own armed forces, and periodic displays of U.S. military power when the Kingdom itself was threatened (Quandt, 1981b). The Saudis also built a substantial military infrastructure far beyond the immediate needs of their own forces. These facilities were vital in facilitating U.S. deployment to the Kingdom during Operations Desert Shield and Desert Storm.

The Saudis considered Israel to be responsible for much of the region's instability. They argued that Arab regimes turned to Moscow for weapons and support because of Israel, making the area more prone to radicalism. In addition, they saw the Palestinian question as a perpetual source of instability in the region (Quandt, 1981b).

The Arab-Israeli crisis complicated U.S. planning and alliance-building in the region. After President Carter declared the Gulf a vital

U.S. interest in 1980, the biggest hurdle for the military proved to be not only meeting the military-logistics challenges but also developing a regional political framework within which the Rapid Deployment Force could function (Kupchan, 1987). Although the Gulf Arabs did share the U.S. commitment to opposing radicalism in the region, they feared that by openly siding with the United States they would lay themselves open to charges of perfidy from the street. As a result, high-profile U.S. diplomatic efforts, such as Secretary of State Alexander Haig's attempts to get the Gulf states to sign onto an anti-Soviet "strategic consensus," often failed.

American planners also considered—but eventually ruled out—Israeli participation in a regional security system. For military reasons, an Israeli role was desirable, since access to its bases was virtually guaranteed, unlike in many Arab states: Domestic politics in host countries rendered access to facilities problematic. Furthermore, Israel has good air defenses and anti-terrorist networks, reducing the vulnerability of U.S. forces deployed there (Kupchan, 1987). The plan to use Israeli facilities was eventually discarded in 1981, however, because Arab leaders viewed it with suspicion, and U.S. planners feared that the use of U.S. forces based in Israel would play into radical Arab or Muslim propaganda against the United States (Johnson, 1984).

When the United States would not sell certain arms systems to the Gulf states, other suppliers eagerly filled the void; the result was increased interoperability and maintenance problems in the region, as well as financial losses to U.S. firms. Saudi Arabia sought British-built Tornados over the F-15, partly because it could base them anywhere in the Kingdom without operating constraints, and it could be ensured of future access to emerging technologies. Furthermore, the Reagan administration's fears of an adverse U.S. domestic reaction led to U.S. firms' losing contracts to supply air forces in the smaller Gulf states, so that there was an even greater diversity of suppliers to the region (Cordesman, 1986).

Arms-sales prohibitions resulted in a lower threshold for committing U.S. forces, reduced the effectiveness of these forces once in place, and led to doubts about U.S. constancy. Less able to defend themselves and less able to work together because of their mélange of military suppliers, Gulf militaries were more likely to call on Washington for even limited threats. In addition, the different types of weapons among the Gulf militaries and the lack of U.S. facilities made an effective U.S. presence harder to establish (Cordesman, 1988).

Furthermore, U.S. signals to Gulf leaders were often confused. On the one hand, U.S. military and diplomatic officials strongly encouraged the Saudis and other Gulf leaders to purchase U.S. equipment to defend the Gulf. On the other hand, congressional restrictions on arms sales to the Gulf reduced confidence about the U.S. ability to provide the necessary assistance. Riyadh's efforts to overbuild its facilities somewhat offset the effect of these problems.

The Gulf states' reluctance to allow the United States to preposition equipment in the region also hindered U.S. attempts to fulfill its security goals in the Persian Gulf. Avoiding a *fait accompli,* either by the Soviets or by a strong regional power such as Iraq, would be far more difficult without prepositioned equipment. Even more important during the Cold War, the United States sought to be able to fight in the Persian Gulf without sacrificing its ability to sustain combat elsewhere, a multifront approach having supply and access problems that would have proven difficult without extensive prepositioning.[2]

Even during crises, U.S. options were limited. During the 1988 reflagging operation, for example, Kuwait would not allow the United States to base military forces there, despite the ongoing U.S. escort operation and Iranian attacks on Kuwaiti tankers and oil facilities.

The ups and downs of the Arab-Israeli dispute track with the Gulf states' willingness to cooperate openly with the United States, resulting in periods during which the Gulf states were more vulnerable. Saudi Arabia halted its move away from the United States, which began when the U.S. recognized Israel, only after negotiations ended the first Arab-Israeli War in 1950. After the 1967 War, Riyadh temporarily reduced ties to the United States. Bahrain severely restricted the U.S. use of its facilities after the October War, limiting the frequency and duration of the docking of U.S. Naval vessels. Following Israel's annexation of the Golan Heights in 1981, then–Crown Prince

---

[2]The above U.S. goals are taken from Wohlstetter, 1980.

Fahd canceled a trip to Washington in protest. After Israel invaded Lebanon in 1982, the Saudis briefly moved again to distance themselves from Washington (Cordesman, 1984; Kupchan, 1987).

U.S. ties to Israel also provided an opportunity for the Soviet Union to expand its influence in the region, and they became a source of division between the United States and its NATO allies. In general, Moscow was able to play on resentment engendered by U.S. support for Israel to gain influence with radical governments and groups. Even China got into the act: Saudi Arabia began acquiring CSS-2 (Dong Feng) missiles from China in late 1987, partly because it was frustrated over the U.S. F-15 sale restrictions (Cordesman, 1988).

The Arab-Israeli dispute also limited the United States' ability to rely on the facilities of its NATO allies. To deploy quickly to the Gulf, the United States needs transit rights, and European allies were nervous about offending Arab sensibilities (Newsom, 1981). Spain denied the use of its bases during the October 1973 War and again in 1979, during the mid-January demonstration deployment of 12 USAF F-15s to Saudi Arabia during the crisis in Iran. Similarly, even though Portugal did not bend under Arab pressures to prohibit U.S. use of the Azores as a stopover during an airlift to resupply Israel during the 1973 War, subsequent Portuguese governments have indicated that the United States would not be permitted access to Lajes air base in the Azores to help counter "Arab interests."[3]

The effect of the Arab-Israeli dispute on Gulf security was not entirely negative. For example, Saudi Arabia and Egypt were embroiled in a war in North Yemen for much of the 1960s. The direct Egyptian role came to an abrupt end after Israel's humiliating defeat of Egyptian forces in the 1967 War. Cairo's need for Saudi assistance in rebuilding its military led it to help broker a peace in Yemen and move to improve relations with Riyadh. Similarly, by punishing the United States with an oil embargo after the 1973 War, Saudi Arabia was able to bolster its domestic credentials as well as its economy.

---

[3]During the 1973 War, Spain quietly allowed aerial tankers based in Spain to refuel American jet fighters being ferried to Israel.

IMPLICATIONS OF U.S. TIES TO ISRAEL DURING DESERT STORM

When Saddam Hussein demanded a resolution of the Palestinian issue as one of his conditions for withdrawing from Kuwait, he tried to change the nature of the dispute from one limited to Iraq and Kuwait to one that encompassed the Palestinian issue—the rallying cry of Arab nationalism for decades. To justify a greater regional role, Iraq had played up its hostility to Israel before the invasion and appeared to be attracting significant public support in Arab countries. On July 1, 1990—a month before Iraq invaded Kuwait—Saddam declared that Iraq now had chemical weapons to deter Israeli nuclear weapons. His subsequent justification of the invasion in terms of the Arab-Israeli issue led many Palestinians to support Kuwait's occupation, alienating leaders in the Gulf and depriving the Palestinians of a major source of financial support. That declaration also led supposedly moderate and pro-Western Arab countries with large Palestinian populations to fear for internal stability should they oppose the invasion; Jordan, for one, chose to side with Saddam to minimize internal unrest.

The Arab-Israeli conflict also figured in the conduct of the war by forcing the United States to defend Israel from Iraq, despite Israel's own impressive capabilities. Iraq attacked Israel in the hope that Israel would respond militarily, weakening or breaking the multinational coalition. Israel did not rise to the bait, primarily because the United States devoted considerable resources to defending Israel. For the United States, however, the possibility of an Israeli entry into the war concerned officials, particularly since Israel would have had to overfly Jordan and Saudi Arabia to strike at Iraq, possibly leading Amman to side even more with Iraq. Moreover, an Israeli strike might have split the coalition (Gordon and Trainor, 1995).

Baghdad attempted to exploit this vulnerability by launching a number of Scud missiles at Israeli urban areas. Fearful that any Israeli retaliation would collapse the delicate political underpinnings of the coalition, enormous political capital was invested in keeping the Israeli armed forces on the sidelines. That coalition air forces expended hundreds of sorties attempting to shut down Iraqi Scud missile operations points to a measurable military effect of the conflict. The air-campaign plan had not envisioned such an intense

"Scud hunt," which diverted those sorties away from other targets of more direct operational value to the war's prosecution. The Iraqi Scuds were never a significant military threat to coalition operations. However, the need to preserve coalition unity led to them being perceived as a high-priority strategic problem that in turn demanded the commitment of sizable resources to their neutralization.[4]

Difficulties Faced by the Air Force As a Result of the Conflict

Several specific logistics difficulties for the U.S. Air Force emerged during Operations Desert Shield and Desert Storm: a lack of advance planning, uncertainties regarding the basing of U.S. forces on the territory of the Gulf states, insufficient regional facilities for crew rest for Air Force personnel, limitations on permissible flight corridors, and inadequate advance information about local facilities. Most of these difficulties stemmed from local political sensitivities to high-visibility cooperation with the United States—sensitivities that were, in part, a result of U.S. ties to Israel.

Contingency planning was limited by the uncertainty that stemmed from the Gulf states' desire to keep their ties to the United States low-profile—further complicating the U.S. deployment. In Europe and Korea, where the United States has formal security agreements, access and deployment details have been worked out in advance, and agreed-upon plans are available for execution in the event of a crisis. Because planning in the Gulf was restricted to less-formal efforts, the United States had fewer "off-the-shelf" plans ready when Iraq invaded. Moreover, the United States did not have host-nation support agreements with such key states as Kuwait and Saudi Arabia. Improvisation and creative thinking enabled the Air Force to work around many of these problems, although at times the Air Force paid a substantial price in efficiency and system stress.

The absence of a complete operational plan was widely regarded as the principal source of the numerous difficulties confronted by the Military Airlift Command (MAC) and the Tactical Airlift Command

---

[4]Some 1,500 sorties were flown against Scud targets, representing 3.6 percent of the total coalition air effort. By comparison, attacks on the Iraqi oil-production, -refining, and -storage infrastructure consumed 1.4 percent of sorties (Keaney and Cohen, 1993, pp. 83–84).

(TAC) during the initial deployment phase of Operation Desert Shield. Neither a published plan nor a Time Phased Force Deployment List (TPFDL) existed when the deployment order was received in August 1990, so both had to be improvised.

Improved Cooperation After Desert Storm

As a result of Desert Storm, problems related to beddown, information on facilities, and prepositioning have lessened, because defense relations have become more explicit and routine. The operation itself provided the United States with better knowledge of the Gulf states and stronger working relations with Gulf officials.

Since Desert Storm, Gulf states have formalized U.S. access to the region, making it easier to deploy larger numbers of forces quickly. Kuwait, Qatar, Bahrain, and the UAE have signed defense cooperation agreements granting the United States access to regional facilities. The agreements with the Gulf states also include combined exercises and prepositioning. As a result, an extensive supply and support network exists today for U.S. forces deployed to the Gulf during a crisis.

Other Outcomes of the Gulf War

The Gulf War also profoundly transformed many of the non-Gulf Arab states. Egypt completed its transition from outcast to leading player in Arab and regional affairs. Egypt's new status became evident when the Arab League moved its headquarters back to Cairo in 1991 and Egypt's foreign minister, Ismet `Abd al-Meguid, was elected as the League's new Secretary-General. For Syria, the war brought an opportunity to halt the economic decline and military erosion caused by the withdrawal of Soviet patronage. The advantages provided by improved political ties to the West and to moderate Arab regimes led Damascus to move toward the Western camp.

Indeed, the Arab-Israeli peace talks began partly as a result of events in the Gulf. Desert Storm removed a major foreign threat from Israel. At the same time, Palestinian support for Iraq led the Gulf states to cut funding and support, leading to a financial crisis and political isolation of Palestinians. Consequently, the PLO leadership was forced to offer better relations with Israel as a way of regaining funding and ending the isolation. The end of the Cold War, which left Syria and the PLO without a major international backer, and the rise of HAMAS as a rival to the PLO also were major factors leading the Palestinians to the peace table.

Chapter Four

CAUTIOUS PROGRESS ON COOPERATION

Whether Israel plays a role in Gulf security depends in large part on the final nature of the Arab-Israeli peace and the resolution of the Palestinian issue. The degree of any peace is not clear at present, and it could range from a "Cold Peace" that involves only limited political recognition to warmer ties that could include security cooperation. Capitalizing on the security benefits of peace will require overcoming opposition both in the Gulf and in Israel.

This chapter begins by noting the tentative nature of the peace process so far and the many hurdles that must be overcome before a comprehensive peace is achieved. It follows this discussion by assessing both the likelihood that the Gulf states will cooperate with Israel on security issues and whether the Israelis might cooperate with the Gulf states if those states were willing to accept Israel as a security partner. The last section of the chapter suggests the reasons that greater cooperation remains a strong possibility—although it may be many years away.

AN UNCERTAIN PEACE

As of this writing, progress on a comprehensive peace between Arabs and Israelis has been promising but limited because of the absence of an Israeli-Syrian peace treaty and continued Israeli-Palestinian hostility. So far, Egypt, the PLO, and Jordan have signed agreements with Israel, and Israel has improved its formal relations with Morocco, Tunisia, Qatar, and Oman. Negotiations with Syria have been contentious in recent months, but a breakthrough may still occur. Over the long term, several Gulf states may also make a formal peace with Israel, especially if Syria and Israel sign a peace treaty.

This study focuses on the optimistic scenario: that the peace process will continue. From the point of view of this study, a "successful" peace process would have the following characteristics:

- The fate of the Palestinians would no longer be a rallying cry throughout the Arab and Muslim world. Presumably, for this to come to pass would require most of the Palestinian people and leadership to be satisfied with the peace agreement—a situation that is currently a long way off.

- Other Arab-Israeli territorial disputes would be resolved satisfactorily. A satisfactory resolution of the Golan Heights is particularly important, but other territorial disputes such as the Israeli "security zone" along its border with Lebanon could prove important. Furthermore, the status of Jerusalem should be resolved in such a manner that all governments will not fear widespread domestic criticism on this issue.

- The "frontline" states of Egypt, Jordan, Syria, and Lebanon all would oppose, or at least not actively seek, the exclusion of Israel from participation in regional political, security, and economic fora.

This definition of *peace* leaves considerable room for future disputes and tension. The fate of Palestinian returnees is likely to be a particularly contentious issue. Progress on territorial disputes, the Palestinian issue, and peace between Israel and its neighbors, however, will solve several of the most pressing problems and will enable Israel to begin playing a greater role in the Gulf.

A comprehensive peace as outlined above may be many years off. The election of Benjamin Netanyahu as Israel's Prime Minister in 1996 and the subsequent violence between the Palestinian Authority and the Israeli government have raised concerns that the peace process will move forward slowly, if at all. Concerns include the following:

- Uncertain implementation of existing agreements.   Many Palestinians and Arab leaders worry that the new Netanyahu government will not honor existing agreements on borders, autonomy, and/or financial assistance, despite statements by Netanyahu to the contrary.

- The fate of Lebanon.   Southern Lebanon remains a war zone where Israel and the Israeli-backed Southern Lebanese Army battle the Islamist militia Hezbollah, which Israel contends could easily be crushed by Syria.   Conflict in Lebanon has the potential to keep hostility toward Israel high in the Arab world and make Israelis reluctant to move forward on any peace.

- The status of the Golan Heights.   During the recent election campaign, Netanyahu and his supporters regularly criticized the Peres government for its supposed willingness to return the strategically important Golan Heights to Syria.   Damascus, for its part, insists on the return of the Golan Heights as a part of any peace agreement.

- A colder peace.   Optimists had hoped that the peace process would do more than stop war between Israel and its neighbors; they also believed that it might lead to trade and, eventually, security cooperation.   The election of Netanyahu suggests that the Israeli government and many Israelis are highly skeptical of such steps.

The concerns are not only about the Israeli government.   Since limited autonomy began in the Gaza Strip and West Bank, divisions within the Palestinian community have been rife.   Yasir Arafat's loyalists have struggled to impose control on radical religious elements led by HAMAS.   Furthermore, broader divisions—such as those between Palestinians who remained in the West Bank and Gaza and those who left—also have the potential to paralyze any Palestinian government.

At the very least, these recent events are likely to slow the peace process.   Breakthroughs in negotiations on contentious issues, such as the level of Palestinian autonomy and the status of the Golan Heights, will prove particularly difficult.   As of this writing, the peace process could stall, move forward slowly, or perhaps even move backward as previous agreements are called into question.

WILL THE GULF STATES INCREASE COOPERATION WITH THE UNITED STATES OR ISRAEL?

Even with such a comprehensive peace, both the Gulf states and Israel will remain cautious about security cooperation in the near term. The Gulf states are likely to fear domestic and regional criticism if they move closer to Israel, and the Israelis are not eager to get involved in potential conflicts far from their borders. In general, it will be difficult to convince the Gulf states that Israel can bring capabilities to the table that the United States cannot and to convince the Israelis to become involved in events that do not directly threaten Israel's security. (See Appendix B for more details on U.S.–Israeli relations today.)

Peace will not eliminate hostility toward the United States in the region. Many Arabs and Muslims are hostile to U.S. values, culture, and policies in the region—a sentiment particularly common among Islamists. Thus, many of the limits on U.S.–Gulf military cooperation stemming from Gulf leaders' domestic political concerns will remain despite progress in relations between Israel and the Arab world.

Islamist groups will remain highly opposed to cooperation with Israel, particularly on security issues. Relying on "infidels" from the United States for the Gulf's security is bad enough for the Islamists, because it suggests the Muslim world's weakness vis-à-vis the West. Bringing in Israel is unthinkable. Some Islamists may even move closer to Iran as a result.

Saudi Arabia is likely to prove especially sensitive to the prospect of more-open ties to Washington or direct ties to Israel. The importance of Islam in the regime's legitimating ideology causes Riyadh to fear criticism from Islamic militants. If the status of Jerusalem remains unresolved, Saudi attitudes toward Israel are likely to change even more slowly. Although the Saudis were grateful for the prompt and forceful U.S. response to the Iraqi challenge, they fear that another major U.S. deployment to the region would bring about a surge in Islamic activism in the Kingdom.[1]   Open relations with Israel would prove even more troublesome.

The smaller Gulf states also are suspicious of Israel. Many Gulf leaders believe that Israel wants to be a regional superpower and are hesitant to engage in even economic cooperation for fear of encouraging Israeli ambitions. Better ties to Israel will take time for the Gulf populace to accept. Even if the peace process leads to peace between states, peace between peoples will take more time.

Neither Iran nor Iraq, the two leading security threats to the Gulf, is a likely signatory to any peace treaty in the near future, and they both probably will seek to capitalize on political friction that springs from peace. As long as Iran remains strongly opposed to a U.S. presence in the region, Saudi Arabia will limit its overt military cooperation with Washington.[2]

The Gulf states are likely to differ among themselves regarding the extent of their ties to Israel. Oman and Qatar—two Gulf states historically suspicious of Riyadh's regional aspirations—are the most likely to lean toward ties to Israel; indeed, they are the ones that have been willing to move closer to Israel on commercial and diplomatic ties so far. If the smaller Gulf states do choose to move ahead on relations with Israel, the Saudis probably would do little more than caution them in private to be careful. However, Saudi Arabia still is the preeminent Gulf state, and none of the others is likely to risk being isolated on such a potentially sensitive issue.

If and when Syria signs a peace treaty with Israel, cooperation between the Gulf states and Israel will become far easier. Riyadh is following Damascus' lead, and the other Gulf states fear being isolated if they move too close to Israel. Yet the potential for closer ties remains. Oman, Bahrain, and Qatar have already received Israeli officials. Kuwait still mistrusts the PLO and King Hussein of Jordan more than it does Israel, and would readily consider cooperating on a

---

[1]One expert noted that, in Desert Storm itself, the large Western troop presence and the pitting of Muslims against Muslims led to the surge in Islamic militancy in the Kingdom in the early 1990s.

[2]One expert noted that, in general, the Saudis seek accommodation rather than confrontation. Thus, they are reluctant to antagonize Iran, which, for geostrategic and ideological reasons, represents a long-term threat to the Kingdom.

variety of issues. Unlike the frontline states of Syria, Jordan, Egypt, and Lebanon, the Gulf states do not have a history of bloodshed that will interfere with better relations.

WILL ISRAEL PARTICIPATE?

Initially, Israelis are likely to resist playing a greater role in Arab affairs. Peace, for many, was to facilitate separation from the Arabs, not to increase Israel's involvement in Arab disputes. In addition, the uncertainties of the peace process make Israelis feel especially vulnerable. Moreover, Israelis might hesitate to become further associated with the United States, particularly in countries whose populations are often hostile to America. So far, Israeli officials in general are reluctant to start combined planning for threats to the Gulf or to otherwise play a direct role there.

If peace between Israel and the Gulf states is similar to that between Egypt and Israel, prospects for increased security cooperation are likely to be limited. Despite peace, the Egyptian government, for reasons stemming from domestic politics, is not willing to engage in high-visibility cooperation with Israel or the United States. Even under Sadat, Egypt remained unwilling to formally provide the United States with a permanent base, although it did informally allow the United States considerable access to its facilities.[3] Direct cooperation between Egypt and Israel has consisted mostly of economic and political ties, with security cooperation being limited to low-visibility matters. For example, in 1977, Israeli intelligence provided Egyptian President Sadat with information about a Libyan plot against him (Spiegel, 1983).

Jordan today offers a more promising model for cooperation. Israel and Amman are considering extensive economic cooperation, and intelligence-sharing is highly likely. Moreover, Israel appears willing to act as a guarantor for Jordan's integrity should Iraq or Syria pose a

---

[3]Egypt's reluctance to clarify arrangements for the use of the Ras Banas base led Congress, in frustration, to temporarily hold up aid in 1983. Because the Egyptian government proved sensitive about a U.S. presence on the ground, the United States quickly withdrew the AWACS planes sent to Egypt to detect hostile Libyan action and toned down the visibility of its forces there (Spiegel, 1983; McNaugher, 1983).

threat to it. Although security ties are not overt, the relationship is, nonetheless, likely to be strong.

The extent of future cooperation depends heavily on the nature of the Syrian-Israeli peace. Saudi Arabia is not likely to move too far ahead of Syria on relations with Israel, and Assad has signaled that he will move slowly on political, economic, and other ties with Israel.[4] The 1996 elections in Israel—during which Netanyahu harshly criticized Peres' government for considering the return of the Golan Heights to Syria in exchange for peace—suggest that many Israelis are apprehensive about negotiations with Assad.

The threat perceived by Israel and by the states of the region will play a large part in determining the extent of possible cooperation. In general, if Israel were attacked during a conflict in the Gulf, incorporating it into a broader coalition would not encounter as strong a resistance from the Gulf states as it did during Desert Storm. If Israel were not attacked, however, Gulf leaders would find such participation harder to justify.

An Iranian threat to the region would be the most likely one to draw in Israel. Leading Israelis across the political spectrum fear that Iran will stir up Islamic militants in the region and develop nuclear weapons. (See Appendix C for a discussion of the effect of weapons of mass destruction on Gulf security.) Similarly, most Gulf leaders see Iran as the greatest threat to their security, particularly over the longer term.

Israel's attitude also will be heavily shaped by U.S. concerns. For Israel to increase its role, Washington initially will have to act as a middleman to allay mutual suspicions. In exchange for cooperating in the Gulf, Israeli officials might seek rewards, such as increased U.S. military aid or new forms of military cooperation and commitment.

In the event of a crisis, Israel is likely to press the United States for guaranteed access to any U.S. equipment prepositioned in Israel. Thus, it may seek a "dual key" arrangement—i.e., one that would al-

---

[4]During the oil embargo, Saudi Arabia's King Faisal repeatedly stressed the importance of an Israeli-Syrian disengagement agreement as part of his conditions (Quandt, 1977).

low Israel to use U.S. equipment prepositioned in Israel during a crisis. Moreover, Israel will want the United States to pay for any equipment stationed there and may ask for compensation for the use of Israeli facilities.

REASONS FOR CAUTIOUS OPTIMISM

Despite many obstructions, some cooperation has occurred between the Gulf states and Israel, leading us to look for other reasons for cautious optimism about peace. Egos, reputations, and expectations are involved in the confrontation with Israel, so change will be slow. But change is nevertheless occurring. Indeed, given that the pace of change in the Gulf is often glacial, a veritable sea change toward Israel can be said to have occurred in the region in recent years, as indicated by Qatari and Omani moves to establish better relations with Israel. In addition, the Gulf states now have the option of working directly with Israel without U.S. mediation. During the multilateral peace talks, which addressed issues such as water rights, economic ties, and arms control, the Gulf states formed direct contacts with Israel. Moreover, the talks have led both Arabs and Israelis to rethink old assumptions and explore the possibility of joint problem-solving.

Many of the sources of pressure against ties to Israel are gone or have diminished. Arab nationalists currently do not pose a great threat to area regimes. Part of the Palestinian leadership has accepted relations with Israel, and the number of Palestinians in the Gulf states was reduced following the Iraqi invasion of Kuwait. Syria, which long opposed Gulf-Israeli cooperation, also is becoming more amenable to relations with Israel.

Although Israelis have not yet sought close security ties with any of the Gulf Arab states, they are not ruling out all forms of cooperation. Israeli defense officials have indicated that they would be willing to allow more U.S. prepositioning to help in Gulf contingencies and would sell arms to the region. During Desert Storm, Israel also offered to provide mine-sweepers.

Direct cooperation already is taking place, although it is primarily limited to economic and diplomatic measures. On December 26, 1994, Israeli Prime Minister Yitzhak Rabin visited Oman, the first public visit by an Israeli leader to an Arab Gulf state ("Israeli Prime Minister Sees Sultan in Oman," December 30, 1994). On January 20, 1995, Enron Corporation signed a letter of intent with the Qatar General Petroleum Corporation to develop a liquid-natural-gas project that might export gas to Israel ("Deal by Enron with Qatar," January 20, 1995).

Over the long term, popular attitudes toward Israel may change. Elsewhere in the Middle East, even many supposed Islamic leaders have accepted working with Israel in practice if not in theory. Establishment clerics in Saudi Arabia, Syria, and Egypt have legalized peace talks between Israel and the Arab states. Whether these attitude changes continue, however, will depend in large part on whether Islamic radicalism fails to flourish in the long term and other, more-temperate ideologies arise to take its place.

This argument for progress on an Arab-Israeli peace is, of course, optimistic. Israel, the Arab states, and the Palestinians all remain highly suspicious of the peace process and are not likely to move quickly, if at all, in coming years. The election of Benjamin Netanyahu in 1996, the continued violence in the Palestinian territories, and the Arab governments' attempts to form a united front on negotiations all suggest that progress on peace will take years and may even move backwards at times as implementation drags.

Progress on peace is necessary if the United States is to gain the full security benefits of an Arab-Israeli peace. As the peace process now stands, Gulf leaders' misgivings about any Israeli role remain high, and the citizens of the Gulf states still view Israel with hostility. For Israel to complete its transformation from a hindrance to the U.S. military in the Persian Gulf to a source of assistance, these misgivings must be overcome.

Chapter Five

THE VALUE OF ISRAELI PARTICIPATION TO THE U.S. AIR FORCE IN THE EVENT OF A CRISIS IN THE REGION

If the peace process can move forward, the security of the Gulf will be enhanced and Air Force operations in the region will face fewer complications. In this chapter, we describe the possible operational military value of Israeli integration into Gulf security affairs. We address four topics, which are ordered roughly according to the visibility of Israeli participation:

- Use of Israeli airspace for overflight

- Indirect Israeli participation in intelligence-sharing, technology and/or equipment transfer, and training

- Access to Israeli air bases and prepositioning

- Direct Israeli participation in combined operations against a regional threat.

We discuss each in turn.

USE OF ISRAELI AIRSPACE

Aerial access to Saudi Arabia and the Arabian peninsula is fairly limited from the west. During Operations Desert Shield and Desert Storm (ODS), most traffic came in through Egyptian airspace as shown in Figure 5.1. This route permits use of an area more than 700

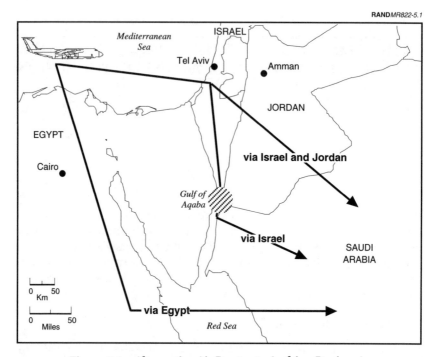

Figure 5.1—Alternative Air Routes to Arabian Peninsula

km across,[1] which gives ample room to shift flights around to avoid bad weather or to maintain multiple corridors.

If access to Egyptian airspace is denied, a route is available that transits only Israeli territory. However, this corridor is extremely narrow, traversing as it does the Gulf of Aqaba, where Israel is barely 5 km wide (the cross-hatched circle in Figure 5.1). There would thus be little margin for error in bad weather, and a high volume of traffic could be sustained only by precisely funneling aircraft through this narrow bottleneck. In addition, the potential for inadvertently violating the border of either Egypt or Jordan would obviously be

---

[1]Approximately the distance from the Israeli-Jordanian-Egyptian border at Elat-Aqaba-Taba to the Egyptian-Sudanese border along a line roughly paralleling the Saudi Red Sea coastline. Egypt has more than 800 km of Mediterranean coastline.

very high, so this route must be considered a last resort if neither Egypt nor Jordan were willing to cooperate.

A more workable alternative to the trans-Egypt route would be one that used both Israeli and Jordanian airspace, a route more than 200 km wide at its narrowest point, Israel's Mediterranean coast.[2]

INDIRECT ISRAELI CONTRIBUTIONS TO GULF SECURITY

Legitimation of Israeli Self-Defense

One potentially significant indirect military benefit of the Arab-Israeli rapprochement would be general recognition by the major Arab countries of Israel's inherent right, as a sovereign state, to self-defense. Absence of this recognition—rooted in a more general Arab perception of Israel's illegitimacy—constituted a possible fracture line in the anti-Iraq coalition of 1991 and forced the coalition to devote considerable resources to defending Israel (see Chapter Four for more details).

Any future conflict in the Gulf is likely to be fought at shorter notice than was Desert Storm, and with fewer forces immediately on hand. Under such circumstances, the diversion of a large number of U.S. sorties to protect Israel could be a major handicap to the United States. Allowing Israel to protect itself—and to retaliate against aggression to the point of itself attacking aggressor air bases, missile launchers, and strategic targets—would remove a potential fault line in future coalition operations and allow U.S. commanders to use their resources to prosecute the war without having to dedicate assets to protect Israel.[3]

---

[2]This route assumes that overflight of the West Bank and Gaza Strip is permitted. If not, air traffic would have to negotiate a bottleneck 30 km or so in width at about 31° 30' north latitude—along a line roughly between Sederot on the eastern edge of Gaza to just south of Idna along the western fringe of the West Bank. How likely such denial would be if both Israel and Jordan were permitting access—or whether any Palestinian authority would be able to monitor, let alone enforce, it—is unknown.

[3]No coalition partner was likely to object to Israel's attempts to shoot down incoming Scuds during the Gulf War; friction was feared if Israel should respond to Iraq's attacks by launching tactically offensive, strategically defensive strikes on, for example, Scud-launch areas in southwestern Iraq. Recognition of Israel as a "normal" state, with all the prerogatives of a normal state, would go a long way toward easing such concerns in the future.

The level of legitimated self-defense depends largely on the extent and warmth of any peace agreement. Given current arrangements, Israel could defend itself and its territory from a direct attack without causing a coalition to fragment. Furthermore, in so doing, it could use coalition information and resources to gather intelligence and coordinate airspace.

If the peace process continues to produce results and to lessen hostility toward Israel, even greater cooperation would be possible. Israel could, in effect, become a tacit coalition partner, flying forward combat air patrols and fighter sweeps over enemy territory.

Equipment and Technology Transfer

In their book *The Generals' War* (1995), Michael Gordon and Bernard Trainor describe the care that was taken to conceal the origin of land-mine-clearing equipment shipped from Israel to Saudi Arabia during Desert Shield.[4] As with the right to self-defense discussed above, the legitimation of Israel in Arab eyes should make such transfers easier to manage in the future.

Table 5.1 lists some major weapon types that Israel has in common with the various GCC states. Since the United States is a major supplier for Israel and most of the Gulf countries, it is not surprising that these equipment inventories overlap substantially. Israeli provision of spare parts and test equipment could be a useful adjunct to efforts aimed at enhancing GCC self-defense capabilities. While it may be difficult to envision direct arms sales from Israel to the Arab world, some technology transfer or sales of modest upgrades and enhancements could follow a comprehensive "warm peace" agreement.

As is clear from Table 5.1, the many items that Israel could provide to the Gulf states are of U.S. manufacture—a situation that puts Israel in a delicate position as a potential competitor with the United States for arms sales and support in the region—something that the United States should discourage. Moreover, U.S. laws prohibit the re-export

---

[4]Measures included repainting the equipment to conceal Israeli markings and altering the flight paths of aircraft carrying it to hide their origin.

Table 5.1

Major Weapon Types Common to Israel and GCC States

Country	Weapon Type
Bahrain	F-16, Sidewinder, Sparrow, M-60, M-113, M-110, TOW, Stinger, Hawk
Kuwait	M-113, M-109, TOW, Hawk, AH-64
Oman	M-60, Sidewinder
Qatar	Stinger
Saudi Arabia	F-15, Sidewinder, Sparrow, Maverick, Hellfire, AH-64, M-60, M-113, M-109, TOW, Stinger, Hawk
UAE	Sidewinder, Hellfire, Hawk

SOURCE: International Institute for Strategic Studies (IISS), *The Military Balance 1994–1995*, London: Pergamon-Brassey's, 1994, pp. 124–141.

of any items of U.S. military equipment provided under Foreign Military Sales, licensing arrangements, or other types of transactions without prior written approval of the U.S. government. Thus, Israeli transfer of weapons to the Gulf Arab states could run afoul of a variety of legalities, and may be something to be done only *in extremis*, and with the explicit concurrence of the United States.

Intelligence-Sharing and Special Operations

There have been reports that one or more Gulf states have already engaged in limited intelligence-sharing with Israel on problems of mutual interest, such as radical Islamic terrorist groups. It is not known how productive these exchanges have been to either side. If Israel has a military confrontation with Iran or Iraq, it could potentially provide useful tactical and strategic intelligence.

Israel's industrial capabilities—including its track record of modifying aircraft for intelligence-gathering and a nascent space-launch capability—give it an ability to deploy "national technical means" unparalleled in the greater Middle East. The Gulf states, on the other hand, have considerable experience keeping tabs on and, in some cases, even supporting, groups that might be seen as common threats both to pro-Western Arab countries and to Israel. They could thus provide information on, for example, personnel and organization that might be difficult for Israel to acquire independently. There may, therefore, be a basis for an expanded set of mutually profitable exchanges in certain areas of intelligence collection and analysis.

Israeli special forces might also contribute covertly to any coalition effort in the Gulf. Such forces might be used to aid the deployment of coalition aircraft and forces, counter enemy air defenses or missile systems, or otherwise assist the overall coalition effort.

ACCESS TO ISRAELI BASES

Israel possesses a fairly large and well-developed air base infrastructure. Figure 5.2 shows the approximate locations of the eight Israeli main operating bases (MOBs) we located in open-source literature.[5] We discuss two aspects of utilizing Israeli bases: distance to likely operating areas in the Gulf and base capacity.

Distance to the Theater

Figure 5.3 compares the distances between various bases and important target areas in Iraq. It reveals that the distance from an Israeli base in the Negev to Baghdad is roughly the same as that from Al Kharj in Saudi Arabia to the Iraqi capital, about 950 km. Flying from an Israeli base against targets in Kuwait would involve about a 2500-km round trip—significantly longer than the distances from Saudi bases, but much shorter than the 3200-km missions regularly flown by F-117s from Khamis Mushait against targets in the Baghdad area in 1991. Finally, the figure shows that targets north of Baghdad, about 700 km away from the Proven Force base at Incirlik, Turkey,

---

[5]All air-base facility data were derived from unclassified extracts from U.S. Defense Mapping Agency, *Air Facility Graphics (AFG)* (not available for public release), n.d., and U.S. Air Force Directorate of Intelligence, and Office of Naval Intelligence, *Airfields and Seaplane Stations of the World* (not available for public release), various issues. Location data are from open-source atlases and maps. It is possible, perhaps even likely, that there are other usable Israeli air bases not listed in these materials.

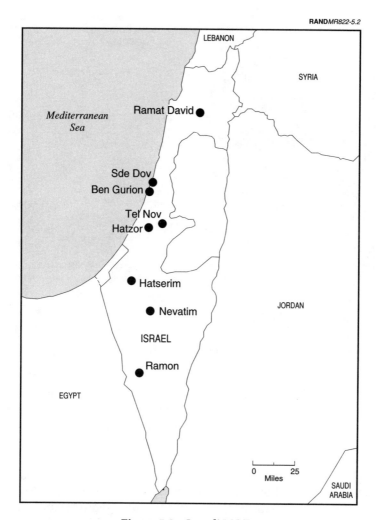

Figure 5.2—Israeli MOBs

are about 1000 km from Israeli MOBs.[6] In sum, distance from likely targets does not rule out the use of Israeli bases in scenarios involving conflict with Iraq.

_____

[6]All distances from Israeli bases assume that overflight of Jordanian territory is allowed. Indeed, in some cases, refueling may need to be performed in Jordanian

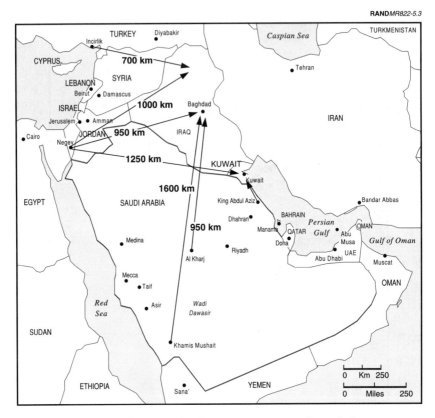

Figure 5.3—Comparative Distances to Target Areas in Iraq

In Figure 5.4, we see something of a different story: The distances depicted are those that would pertain to a conflict with Iran. Because of Iran's size, range-to-target is considerably greater from bases in both Israel and the Gulf states. Of the non-Turkish bases shown, Dhahran, at 1100 km, is the closest to Tehran. Israeli bases, the farthest away, are 1650 km distant.

Two points stand out from this figure. First, Israeli bases are a prohibitively long distance from the Strait of Hormuz, which will likely

---

airspace. Without overflight of Jordan, the utility of Israeli installations for fighter-bomber basing becomes highly questionable across the board.

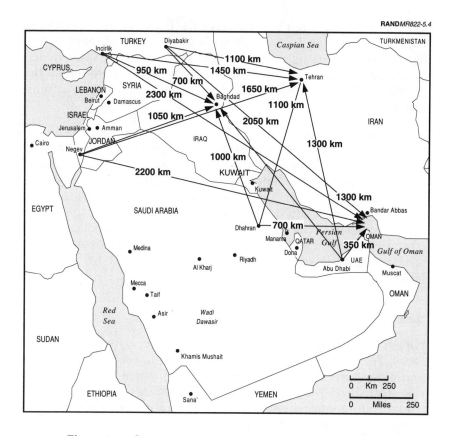

Figure 5.4—Comparative Distances to Target Areas in Iran

be a key battleground of any conflict with Iran. Bases in Oman and the UAE have obvious advantages for providing coverage of the Strait, but even Dhahran in central Saudi Arabia is about 1500 km closer to Hormuz than are Israeli installations (700 km versus 2200 km); even Al Kharj, in central Saudi Arabia, is only 1350 km from the Strait.

Second, bases in Turkey—particularly those in the eastern part of the country, such as Diyabakir—could be very useful in a campaign against Iran, especially against targets in the northern part of Iran and along the Iran-Iraq border.[7] Like the Israeli facilities, however, these bases are too far away from Hormuz to be of much use to fighter-bombers trying to operate in the vicinity of the Strait; hence, even a combination of Israeli and Turkish bases would not suffice to effectively employ land-based air power against Iran in most scenarios.[8]

The longer distances between bases in Israel and targets in the Persian Gulf might prove a blessing in the event of a true nightmare scenario: conflict with a weapon of mass destruction (WMD)-armed foe in the Gulf. This challenge would require greater dispersal of U.S. forces and bases farther from the theater, and would be harder for a foe to target successfully. Under these circumstances, the operational inconveniences associated with longer flights (reduced sortie rates, increased manning requirements, etc.) would be more than offset by the additional security afforded by more-remote operating locations.[9]

Base Capacity

We collected data from open sources on main operating bases in Israel, Turkey, and on the Arabian peninsula. Table 5.2 lists some important bases used in the 1991 Gulf War, along with certain key characteristics. For comparison purposes, Table 5.3 shows similar data for all identified Israeli MOBs, and Table 5.4 tallies the total ramp space—a crude measure of air base capacity—available in Israel, Turkey, and the GCC countries.

---

[7]Overflight of Syria is useful for operations out of central Turkish bases, such as Incirlik, against targets in either Iran or Iraq; the distances shown in the figure assume that overflight is possible. Lack of access to Syrian airspace would not preclude operations from Turkish bases; sorties would, however, be longer in both time and distance.

[8]Bases in Pakistan could be useful for operations over and around the Strait of Hormuz. This study did not assess the number, quality, or availability of Pakistani installations.

[9]This would be even more true if, in the future, Israel fielded ballistic-missile defenses that afforded a degree of protection to all or most of its territory.

Table 5.2

Data on Key Bases Used in Operation Desert Storm

Base	Ramp Area (sq ft)	Longest Runway (ft)	Shelter Area (sq ft)	Shelters	Revetments
Dhahran	12,008,017	12,008	225,261	13	2
Jiddah	9,262,612	10,499	226,432	11	3
Al Karj	5,908,078	13,288	0	0	1
Khamis Mushait	3,629,278	12,467	454,657	46	30
Taif	3,592,900	12,254	267,400	14	0
Incirlik	3,200,108	10,000	277,794	40	0
Tabuk	807,628	10,991	181,216	21	0

Table 5.3

Data on Israeli MOBs

Base	Ramp Space (sq ft)	Longest Runway (ft)	Shelter Area	Shelters	Revetments
Ben Gurion	4,540,750	11,998	191,670	8	0
Hatserim	2,500,496	7,875	525,500	19	36
Tel Nov	1,757,450	7,070	457,200	12	11
Nevatim	1,169,930	10,980	106,272	13	2
Ovda	1,029,136	9,843	236,160	60	10
Ramat David	1,001,125	8,448	555,200	35	0
Hatzor	912,254	8,038	369,459	17	8
Ramon	789,476	10,045	315,035	71	10
Palmachim	601,740	7,874	10,850	1	0
Sde Dov	629,044	5,741	31,050	3	0
U Michaeli	542,150	4,232	25,000	3	1

Table 5.4

Total Ramp Space by Country

Country	Ramp Area (million sq ft)
Saudi Arabia	74.1
Turkey	22.9
Israel	16.1
UAE	15.7
Oman	9.1
Diego Garcia	4.1
Bahrain	2.9
Qatar	2.6
Kuwait	1.8

In looking at these tables, we see several noteworthy features:

- Saudi Arabia alone has more ramp space than all the other listed countries combined.

- In fact, a single Saudi base—Dhahran Airfield—has almost 75 percent of the ramp space of all Israeli MOBs combined (12 million versus 16.1 million square feet).

- Nonetheless, among likely hosts for U.S. forces in the region, only Saudi Arabia and Turkey own more ramp space than Israel.

- Israeli bases are well-equipped with shelters and revetments to protect aircraft: Only Turkey has more shelters, only Turkey and Saudi Arabia have more shelter space, and Israel has the largest number of permanent revetments.[10]

What does this tell us about the ability of Israeli MOBs to supplement or replace bases in the Gulf region proper?

We used rough USAF planning factors to calculate the amount of ramp space needed by the U.S. fixed-wing assets deployed to the

---

[10]Obviously, most of these protective structures are probably filled with Israeli aircraft. However, it does not seem out of the question that some particularly high-value U.S. aircraft—such as F-117s—could "borrow" some shelters if Israel was involved in a future Gulf contingency.

Arabian peninsula during the 1991 Gulf War, which was roughly 38.4 million square feet.[11] As Table 5.5 shows, more than 60 percent of that space—some 23.5 million square feet—was at Saudi bases. Clearly, Israel, with only 16.1 million square feet of total ramp space, could not accommodate nearly as large a force as was deployed to Saudi Arabia in 1990–1991.

To estimate what size force might be hosted on Israeli bases, we calculated—again using USAF planning factors—how much space the Israeli Air Force (IAF) would require for its own assets. Based on open-source order-of-battle information, that figure is about 10.1 million square feet.[12] Thus, at most 6 million square feet would be available for receiving U.S. forces, or only about one-sixth of a "Desert Storm equivalent." Table 5.6 shows two alternative forces— one consisting mainly of bombers, the other primarily of fighters and fighter-bombers—that could be accommodated in that much space.[13]

Table 5.5

Ramp Space Used in Operation Desert Shield/Storm

Country	Ramp Use	Percentage
Saudi Arabia	23,558,023	61.4
Oman	6,269,638	16.3
UAE	5,602,184	14.6
Bahrain	2,457,478	6.4
Qatar	494,614	1.3
TOTAL	38,381,937	

---

[11]This figure includes the parking space needed for each aircraft, along with room required for maintenance, ground maneuver, etc. Planning factors are from USAF document AFH 32-1084, July 1995 draft, specifically paragraph 2.19.

[12]This estimate includes both fixed- and rotary-wing aircraft.

[13]These estimates make no allowances for rotary-wing aircraft or, more important, for strategic airlift operations, which can consume prodigious amounts of ramp space. There are also important operational costs associated with basing aircraft in small groups across a number of bases. Finally, the parking-space requirements used in these calculations do not account for tactical dispersion of aircraft as a hedge against air or missile attack on the base. As such, the examples probably represent an upper bound on the possible force size deployable to Israeli bases, at least those identifiable in unclassified sources.

Table 5.6

Example of Forces Deployable to Israeli Bases

Bomber Force		Ramp	Fighter Force		Ramp
Type	Qty	(sq ft)	Type	Qty	(sq ft)
B-1B	36	2,595,687	F-15C	96	1,153,422
B-2A	16	664,608	F-15E	48	576,711
KC-135	12	748,228	F-16	96	659,485
C-130	12	554,135	A-10	24	323,638
E-3	4	311,885	E-3	4	311,885
E-8	4	311,885	E-8	4	311,885
			KC-135	18	1,122,342
			C-130	12	554,135
TOTAL		5,186,428			5,013,503

From even these rough estimates, it seems clear that *Israeli bases could provide only a partial substitute for facilities in Saudi Arabia and elsewhere on the Arabian peninsula.* The infrastructure in Saudi Arabia in particular is so vast that it would be challenging—although not impossible—to cope with denial of its bases alone, even if the other Gulf states, Israel, and Turkey permitted access. Israeli bases, however, could serve as a limited complement to other facilities.

Prepositioning in Israel

A final aspect of base access in Israel concerns the potential to preposition equipment and supplies there for use in a Gulf contingency.[14]

The United States has prepositioned a significant amount of materiel aboard ships and, especially, ashore in the Gulf. For the USAF, thousands of tons of ammunition, hundreds of vehicles, and several dozen bare-base kits are stored at sites in several Gulf countries, and

---

[14]The importance of prepositioning might be reduced if only precision munitions were used, because the tonnage required would be reduced. On the other hand, having assured access to appropriate types of aviation fuel might be extremely valuable.

there are plans to significantly expand prepositioning in those countries.[15]

Putting equipment and supplies in Israel would seem to make the most sense for supporting operations from there; the transportation burden of moving stocks from Israel to, say, Saudi Arabia would seem to offset much of the advantage conferred by prepositioning in the first place. Financial costs must also be considered. First, it could be expensive simply to move existing stocks from the Gulf states to Israel. Second, some of the governments in the Gulf region contribute toward the cost of maintaining the prepositioning sites.[16] It seems unlikely that they would continue to subsidize stockpiles that were relocated to Israel, and the Israeli government is not likely to pick up all or even part of the tab.

However, as will become clearer when we examine crisis scenarios, the value of Israel as a prepositioning site would increase enormously should other bases in the region be denied to U.S. forces. Israel could not replace Saudi Arabia should facilities in the Kingdom become unavailable, but it would help to offset the loss. Similarly, Israel would provide facilities that are well-defended, thus ensuring they will be available in the event of a crisis.

ISRAEL AS A COALITION PARTNER

Of course, the most ambitious objective of U.S. policy in the wake of any general Arab-Israeli peace agreement would be to facilitate the direct involvement of Israel as a partner in any future Gulf contingency. What capabilities could the IAF in particular bring to bear?

Table 5.7 lists the current IAF combat-aircraft order of battle based on unclassified sources; it shows 488 frontline combat aircraft, 274 of

---

[15]For example, plans are to position enough HARVEST FALCON base-basing equipment to support 55,000 personnel and 750 aircraft at 14 locations (Briefing, U.S. Central Command, Air Forces, "USCENTAF Logistics," July 1995).

[16] Between August 1994 and July 1995, the Gulf states paid $94.4 million of aid-in-kind to support U.S. prepositioning on the peninsula.

Table 5.7

IAF Order of Battle[a]

Type	Quantity
F-16	209
F-4	114
F-15	65
A-4	64
Kfir	36

SOURCE: IISS, *The Military Balance 1994–1995*, London: Pergamon-Brassey's, 1994, pp. 131–132.

[a]Some additional 250 aircraft (120 Kfir and 130 A-4) are in storage.

which are F-15 and F-16 fighters. Furthermore, 50 of the F-4s have been modified to *Phantom 2000* standard by Israel Aircraft Industries; these aircraft have structural improvements, new avionics, and other changes that make them considerably more capable than their F-4E predecessors. Deliveries of these aircraft continue, and eventually the entire F-4 fleet is to be upgraded. In the next few years, the IAF also plans to add more F-15s to its structure, including the F-15I multi-role attack variant.[17]

The IAF, then, fields nearly five wing-equivalents of fighter-bomber aircraft.[18] Its F-15 force gives Israel a high-quality all-weather air-superiority fighter; the IAF has also employed the F-16 extensively as an air-to-air platform. The F-16 also serves the IAF as a strike aircraft, as demonstrated in the Israeli raid on the Iraqi nuclear facility at Osirak in 1981. The most obvious piece missing from the IAF in-

---

[17]The F-15I is a somewhat "detuned" version of the USAF F-15E Strike Eagle. While the F-15E's low-altitude navigation and targeting system, LANTIRN, is not included in the sale, published reports indicate that the Israelis will equip the aircraft with an indigenous system of similar capabilities.

[18]These 488 aircraft appear to be the IAF equivalent of the USAF total aircraft inventory (TAI). The usual rule of thumb is that 100 TAI equate to one 72 primary-aircraft-authorized (PAA) fighter wing-equivalent.

ventory is a long-range, all-weather attack aircraft, a shortcoming that should be rectified with the acquisition of the F-15I.[19]

The IAF, then, could make some contribution in a conflict against a Gulf aggressor. As noted above, geography makes it more suited to operations against Iraq than against Iran, and some support from the United States—especially air-to-air refueling—would likely be needed to maximize its effectiveness. Constraints on Israeli operations would likely include low sortie rates caused by the long distances between IAF bases and likely target areas and a shortage of 24-hour air-to-ground precision-strike capability, even after the F-15I enters service.

The best use for IAF assets might be to employ air-to-air F-15s to bolster coalition capabilities over, say, western Iraq and to use air-to-ground F-16s to strike targets in the same area.[20]

---

[19]The lack of long-range strike capability is perfectly commensurate with the IAF's focus on operations against its main regional antagonists, who have historically been its next-door neighbors. Should successful peace arrangements be achieved with these countries, and as other potential antagonists (such as Iran) acquire longer offensive reach with ballistic missiles, the IAF's need for a more robust power-projection capability may increase.

[20]Obviously, basing Israeli forces in the Gulf region itself would help ameliorate some of these problems. As we see when discussing potential Israeli contributions to the seven crisis scenarios we present in Chapter Six, those cases in which Israel brings the most to the table are precisely those in which, for one reason or another, U.S. access to bases in the Gulf is denied or severely restricted. Under such circumstances, it seems highly unlikely that Israeli forces would be welcome, or able, to operate from installations denied to the United States. The IAF also has no experience operating as an expeditionary force, the requirements for which are much greater than just being able to move airplanes and pilots onto foreign soil. For both these reasons, then, we do not treat the possibility of Israeli air operations from Gulf bases.

Chapter Six

SCENARIOS POTENTIALLY INVOLVING A U.S. MILITARY RESPONSE

The Middle East, including the Persian Gulf region, has long been an area of often-violent instability. Several major events in the region—including the Iranian revolution, the outbreak of the Iran-Iraq War, and the Iraqi invasion of Kuwait—have caught many analysts by surprise. Thus, U.S. military forces must be prepared for a wide range of scenarios. In this chapter, we explore a variety of possible future Middle East conflict scenarios and suggest how an Arab-Israeli peace might affect U.S. operations in the Gulf in each case.

We have organized our analysis around seven scenarios:[1]

- Enforcing demilitarized ("red-line") zones inside Iraq

- Defending Kuwait and Saudi Arabia against Iraq

- Defending Saudi Arabia against a coordinated Iraqi-Yemeni attack

- Defending against an Iraqi-Yemeni attack and Iranian opportunism

- Defending the peninsula littoral against Iran

---

[1]A crucial variable in several of these scenarios, particularly those involving large-scale aggression against Saudi Arabia, will be the possible presence of nuclear weapons or other weapons of mass destruction in the Iraqi or Iranian arsenals. The descriptions that follow do not explicitly address this variable. However, planners should bear this possibility in mind as they sort through the cases below. Appendix C discusses some issues relating to nuclear, biological, and chemical (NBC) weapons in future Gulf crises.

- Helping the Al Saud cope with internal instability
- Deterring Iran in the event of an Iraqi collapse.

These scenarios are a set of plausible events that provide a wide range of challenges to U.S. capabilities. They are to be viewed as heuristics, leading to thoughts and discussions about how an Arab-Israeli peace might affect events in the Gulf. We do not intend these scenarios to be predictive in either a strong (the events detailed *will* happen) or weak (the events *are the most likely* to happen) sense.

This chapter sketches each scenario and a baseline U.S. response (CENTCOM tasking) to each. All are cast in or around the year 2000, and the force structures used reflect current plans and assessments for that time. Uncertainties as to U.S. and foreign capabilities have been resolved according to our best judgment. Each scenario concludes by illustrating how an Israeli role would prove useful in the event of a crisis.

We conclude our discussion of Israel's potential military contribution by attempting to link these seven scenarios with four of the areas of possible cooperation covered in Chapter Five: access to Israeli airspace, access to Israeli air bases, prepositioning in Israel, and use of Israeli air forces.[2] Figure 6.1 summarizes our findings in the form of a "stoplight" chart.

ENFORCING A "RED LINE" WITHOUT SAUDI BASES

Scenario Description

On July 14, 1998—the 40th anniversary of the Iraqi revolution—Saddam Hussein announces that Iraq will never yield to intimidation about its territorial integrity. Iraqi troops, including a Republican Guard division, begin assembling just north of the 32nd Parallel. The U.S. government had previously declared the area south of the 32nd

---

[2]We exclude the indirect contributions, such as intelligence-sharing, because their value is mainly in the longer-term, day-to-day operations of the various militaries as opposed to during crises. Such links as are established will, of course, be invaluable in a conflict in the Gulf, and the product of such processes—for example, improved intelligence, better-trained forces—will have major payoffs if the United States is again called upon to employ force in the region.

RAND*MR822-6.1*

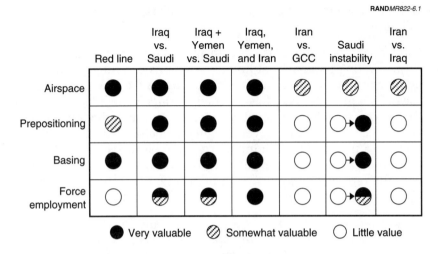

	Red line	Iraq vs. Saudi	Iraq + Yemen vs. Saudi	Iraq, Yemen, and Iran	Iran vs. GCC	Saudi instability	Iran vs. Iraq
Airspace	●	●	●	●	◍	◍	◍
Prepositioning	◍	●	●	●	○	○→●	○
Basing	●	●	●	●	○	○→●	○
Force employment	○	◍	◍	●	○	○→◍	○

● Very valuable   ◍ Somewhat valuable   ○ Little value

Figure 6.1—Value of Israeli Contributions Across Scenarios

Parallel to be a "red line"—a demilitarized area that was off-limits to Iraqi military forces. Reports by U.S. intelligence say that supply and other logistics networks are being assembled in a manner consistent with a move south. However, intelligence does not believe that the size of the deployment is consistent with plans to move forces into Kuwait or Saudi Arabia. The apparent mobilization continues despite U.S. warnings to desist.

Baghdad is willing to challenge the United States for several reasons. It judges that challenging the West along the 32nd Parallel will not provoke a unified-coalition response, and it hopes to split off more-sympathetic coalition members in both Europe and the Arab world from the United States. In Saddam's opinion, most states would support his right to exercise authority within his country's borders. In addition, by repeatedly deploying below the 32-degree-north latitude line, Baghdad hopes to exhaust U.S. patience and resources. Because Iraq can easily send forces south, whereas major U.S. deployments are expensive, time-consuming, and politically difficult, Iraq estimates that repeating such maneuvers will wear down the will of the United States. As an added incentive, by successfully baiting the United States, Saddam might shore up his credibility in the Arab world as a leader willing to challenge the West, even if he is defeated militarily.

Saddam also is trying to use foreign aggression to bolster his steadily disintegrating popularity at home. Sanctions and international isolation continue to wear away at the regime, and a recent increase in the official price of bread has touched off riots in Baghdad and Basra that have had to be put down with force. Although the information cannot be corroborated, several regime defectors report unsuccessful coup attempts by senior military and intelligence leaders, the very core upon whom Saddam relies to remain in power. Concurrent with the reports has come an announcement that the Iraqi head of intelligence died in a helicopter accident, along with two generals.

Concerned about the level of Iraqi activity and intent on enforcing the U.N.'s decision, the United States requests access to several air bases and ports in the Gulf. Kuwait, Oman, and the UAE offer facilities to U.S. forces. The UAE, however, insists that it will not allow combat operations to be conducted out of its territory.

Riyadh, Bahrain, and Qatar refuse U.S. forces access altogether. Riyadh does not believe that Iraqi deployments south of the 32nd Parallel pose a serious threat to its security—an argument it cited when it requested that the United States not use its bases to carry out Operation Southern Watch, leading to the cancellation of that operation. In general, Saudi Arabia is steadily becoming more opposed to the U.S. campaign to unseat Saddam, because continuing Iranian belligerence is leading Riyadh to be more and more concerned about Iranian intentions and the need for a strong Iraq to counterbalance Tehran. Moreover, both Islamic and nationalist critics in the Kingdom oppose a U.S. deployment in the region, and the regime fears undermining its already-shrinking popularity. Islamists, in particular, argue against greater ties to the West, particularly to coerce another Muslim nation. Bahrain and Qatar might have been willing to provide the United States with bases, but they fear moving ahead of Saudi Arabia on such a potentially volatile issue.

The operation will have to consist of as small a presence as possible. Since Kuwait, Oman, and Israel may be the only three states supporting the U.S. effort, area leaders and U.S. officials are concerned that the operation will damage U.S. credibility in the region (see Figure 6.2).

CENTCOM Tasking

The U.S. National Command Authority (NCA) decides to deploy forces to the Gulf region to

- enforce Iraqi compliance with the Security Council's "red line" (the 32nd Parallel)

RAND*MR822-6.2*

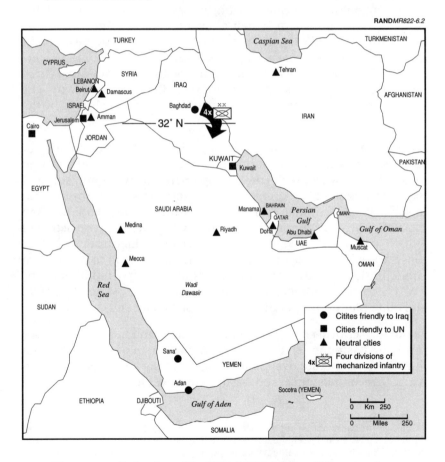

Figure 6.2—Enforcing a "Red Line" Without Saudi Cooperation

- deter and, if necessary, defeat Iraqi aggression against any of its neighbors.

On the peninsula, basing is available only in Kuwait and Oman. Forces can also be deployed into Egypt and Israel.

The Potential Military Value of Israeli Assistance

The dilemma faced in this scenario is how to deploy a credible deterrent and punitive force into the region, with access only to Kuwait and Oman on the peninsula. As long as Egypt is cooperating with the United States, access to Israeli airspace is of only limited value. Access to bases and prepositioned stocks in Israel would be a significant help, however. Assuming overflight of Jordan, some longer-range strike assets, such as F-15Es, could be based in Israel and could be supported by tankers and other assets flying out of Egypt. The rapid employment of these forces would be greatly facilitated by the prepositioning of munitions in Israel or access to Israeli stockpiles.

A composite wing made up of F-15E, F-15C, and F-16C aircraft (for strike, escort, and defense-suppression, respectively) could be based in Israel[3] and tasked with conducting operations west and south of Baghdad, about a 1000-km radius from their bases. This would result in sortie lengths similar to those flown from central Saudi bases in the 1991 Gulf War. Another composite wing, perhaps consisting of A-10, F-15C, and F-16C aircraft, could bed down in Kuwait and cover those areas in southeastern Iraq that are impractical to reach from Israel. In this scenario, operations would be supported by tankers, AWACS, the Joint Surveillance Target Attack Radar System (JSTARS), and other platforms operating from Egypt, Oman, and the UAE.

As noted, a critical constraint in this scenario, and indeed in all cases involving basing in Israel, is access to Jordanian airspace. Without the ability to operate over Saudi Arabia, it may be necessary to run AWACS, reconnaissance, and tanker orbits over Jordan.

---

[3]Although probably not all at one base, complicating logistics and mission planning. It might be possible to lessen the former burden by basing USAF aircraft types at bases hosting IAF units flying the same type, e.g., putting USAF F-16s at an IAF F-16 base.

Israeli forces could play an important role in this scenario because of the U.S. NCA's desire to deploy as small a force as possible and because of the tight basing constraints imposed. Israeli forces could be of particular use in helping maintain combat air patrol (CAP) stations over Jordan to protect both friendly assets operating over Saudi Arabia and Jordan itself against possible Iraqi attack. However, the relative dearth of long-range attack platforms in the IAF inventory, along with the Israelis' doctrinal and training focus on shorter-range operations, puts something of an upper bound on their direct contributions.

DEFENDING KUWAIT AND SAUDI ARABIA AGAINST IRAQ

Scenario Description

In 1997, the United Nations ends sanctions against Iraq. Although Baghdad immediately begins reassembling its missile, WMD, and conventional programs, U.N. Security Council members are reluctant to reimpose sanctions, citing humanitarian concerns. The permanent members are divided, because several Security Council members are eager to continue trade with Iraq, particularly since the military sectors of their economies are desperate for exports to make up for a drop in domestic demand.

Iraq invests most of its renewed oil revenue in rebuilding its military. Although it does not return its army to Desert Storm levels, it does pursue qualitative improvements in all areas. Perhaps even more important, Saddam Hussein reduces the level of politicization in the armed services (although it remains high by Western standards), appointing more-competent officers who seem more concerned with training and planning than their predecessors.

By the year 2000, Iraq's military has returned to near–Desert Storm levels in many areas. Iraq has a sizable number of top-line fighters and fighter-bombers, including F-1s, MiG-29s, and Su-24s. Intelligence suggests that Iraq has rebuilt a large amount of its chemical weapons inventory; it now may have the largest in the Third World. Having learned from Desert Storm, Iraq has built large numbers of mobile erector-launchers for its *al-Hussein* and *al-Hijrah* missiles, both of which are capable of reaching Israel and Riyadh. Iraq's biological-weapons facilities also may be active.

Saddam Hussein's regime remains highly unpopular at home, and he hopes that foreign aggression might rally disaffected Iraqis. Saddam's military investments have not enabled him to rebuild Iraq's economy, which was shattered by the imposition of comprehensive sanctions. As a result, popular resentment of the regime also is increasing. In particular, he is concerned about the loyalty of the armed forces and the intelligence services—key pillars of the regime—which are growing restive under his rule.

The Iraqi invasion, spearheaded by five heavy divisions moving on three axes of advance, catches early-deploying U.S. forces in Kuwait ill-prepared. Elements of the 24th Infantry (Mechanized) and the 82nd Airborne conduct an ad hoc fighting retreat along the coastal highway while forward-deployed Kuwaiti and Saudi forces collapse. The Kuwait and Saudi forces claim they were subjected to attack by chemical weapons. Six second-echelon Iraqi divisions are moving behind the lead forces, which appear poised to overrun Kuwait and much of Saudi Arabia in a matter of days. (See Figure 6.3.)

CENTCOM Tasking

The U.S. National Command Authority orders USCENTCOM to

- secure the necessary bases for conducting defensive and offensive operations on the Arabian peninsula

- halt the Iraqi offensive before key objectives—including oil facilities and important political targets—can be occupied

- expel Iraqi forces from all occupied territory and comprehensively defeat them

- destroy Iraqi WMD facilities, stocks, and delivery systems

- execute measures to prompt or hasten the downfall of the regime in Baghdad.

Because of the fast-moving Iraqi offensive and the potential ballistic-missile threat, bases north of the 20-degree-north latitude line on the Arabian peninsula are not to be used.

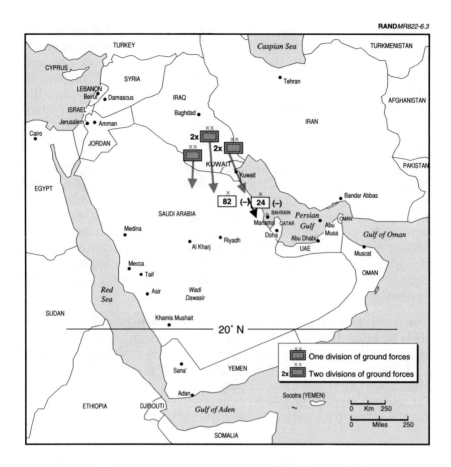

Figure 6.3—Iraqi Attack on Kuwait and Saudi Arabia

The Potential Military Value of Israeli Assistance

This scenario presents several challenges to the USAF. First and foremost, the prohibition of basing north of 20 degrees latitude means that most of the largest Saudi bases cannot be used. In addition, those installations that are still accessible will be quite crowded to begin with, assuming that (1) the Royal Saudi Air Force (RSAF) and

Kuwaiti air force are also withdrawing from bases in the path of the Iraqi onslaught, and (2) the Gulf end of the "air bridge" from the United States will be using many of the same bases that are generating combat sorties. In this case, opening Israeli airspace to U.S. overflight could provide additional routes of ingress into the peninsula. Use of Israeli bases for crew rest and airlifter refueling also could reduce the strain on available bases in the Gulf and increase flow into the theater.[4]

Using Israeli bases as locations from which to strike targets in the same areas as in the preceding scenario (in and around Baghdad and to the south and west of the Iraqi capital) would aid in mounting an interdiction campaign against attacking Iraqi forces, as well as beginning the destruction of Iraq's war-supporting infrastructure—allowing the forces in the Gulf region itself to concentrate on halting the advancing enemy forces.[5] Increased prepositioning in Israel in this scenario would fill the need to begin mounting high-tempo operations very rapidly.

The main value of Israeli forces in this scenario may be in defending their homeland against Iraqi strikes. Here, the legitimation of Israel's right to self-defense may incur great payoffs by enabling U.S. forces to focus on defeating the adversary rather than shielding Israel. Hence, we rate Israeli force employment as very high-value in Figure 6.1, even though their role in general coalition operations may be fairly minimal (lack of long-range platforms, training, doctrine).

---

[4]Given the unstable situation in Saudi Arabia, it might be desirable for strategic-airlift aircraft to land there, drop off their cargoes, then quickly depart to refuel somewhere else more out of the immediate line of fire. Airlifters consume enormous quantities of fuel, however, so a careful analysis of fuel storage, pumping, and resupply at Israeli bases should be undertaken before assuming that Israel would be a practical alternative to other sites for this purpose.

[5]In this scenario, long-range bombers flying from bases in the United States, Europe, and Diego Garcia, could be enormously valuable if they were equipped with munitions that enabled them to effectively attack moving armored formations. See, for example, D. Frelinger, J.S. Kvitky, G. Liberson, C. Neerdaels, *Bomber Flexibility Study: A Progress Report*, Santa Monica, Calif.: RAND, DB-109-AF, 1994, and G. C. Buchan and D. Frelinger, *Providing an Effective Bomber Force for the Future*, Santa Monica, Calif.: RAND, CT-119, 1994. Basing in Turkey such as that afforded to Proven Force in 1991 would also be very helpful in this scenario.

COORDINATED IRAQI-YEMENI ATTACK ON SAUDI ARABIA

Scenario Description

Even after the lifting of U.N. sanctions, Iraq's economy and domestic politics remain troubled. Meanwhile, the long-standing border dispute between Yemen and Saudi Arabia has heated up. Recognizing their common foe, Sana' and Baghdad agree to assault Saudi Arabia on two fronts. In exchange for tying down Saudi forces in the Asir,[6] Yemen will share part of the proceeds from captured Saudi oil production, receive postwar military assistance from Baghdad, and regain territory it considers to be Yemeni.

Saddam Hussein's regime remains highly unpopular at home, and he hopes that aggression on foreign soil might rally disaffected Iraqis. Because he has focused on rebuilding the military, Saddam has not been able to reconstruct the Iraqi economy, which has been shattered by the imposition of comprehensive sanctions for seven years. As a result, popular resentment of the regime also is increasing. In particular, Saddam is concerned about the loyalty of the armed forces and the intelligence services—key pillars of the regime—which are growing restive under his rule.

Yemen's President Ali Abdallah Salih faces similar challenges. Yemen's economy is provoking widespread discontent. Since Desert Storm, Yemenis no longer enjoy favored status as workers in Saudi Arabia, which prompted hundreds of thousands of Yemenis to return home, sending the unemployment rate soaring. At the same time, the discovery of oil near the Saudi-Yemeni border prompted high popular expectations of imminent riches, but difficulties getting the supplies into production have led to disappointed expectations. Concerned about continuing disaffection among southerners and northern tribesmen, Salih has lavished (by Yemeni standards) money on the armed services to ensure their loyalty and ability to suppress dissent.

---

[6]Yemen lost control over a buffer area in the Asir (part of which may be rich in oil) to Ibn Saud in the early 1930s, and Yemeni leaders have periodically voiced their dissatisfaction with this situation.

Salih is trying to use the campaign against the Saudis, who are a traditional enemy for many northern Yemenis, to rally his citizens. Many Yemenis resent the Al Saud's meddling in Yemeni affairs and Riyadh's curtailment of Yemeni work permits since Desert Storm. Salih hopes to rekindle the nationalist sentiment that had shattered in the violence of the 1994 civil war. More practically, he hopes to regain territory in the Asir region, particularly the part that may be rich in oil. Moreover, several Yemeni oil fields are in an area claimed by Saudi Arabia, and oil producers have been reluctant to develop those fields for fear of offending Riyadh. In the weeks before the crisis, Yemeni and Saudi forces have skirmished along the border, resulting in several dozen casualties.

Taking advantage of a period of political uncertainty in Riyadh—the King lies gravely ill—the two conspirators strike quickly and with little warning. Early-deploying U.S. forces fall in on prepositioned equipment in Kuwait and fight a fierce defensive battle along the coastal highway, but are flanked by strong Iraqi forces moving inland. On the other front, several brigade-sized Yemeni mechanized task forces strike out up the Red Sea coast and inland toward Wadi Dawasir (see Figure 6.4). Although the Yemeni thrusts are weak, so too are the local defenses, and Saudi forces fall back in disarray on all fronts. Key installations along the Yemeni-Saudi border are denied to deploying U.S. forces as a result.

CENTCOM Tasking

The U.S. National Command Authority orders USCENTCOM to

- secure the necessary bases for conducting defensive and offensive operations on the Arabian peninsula

- halt the Iraqi and Yemeni offensives before key objectives—including oil facilities and important political targets—can be occupied

- expel enemy forces from all occupied territory and comprehensively defeat them.

Because of the threat from the multiple prongs of the combined offensive, no bases in Kuwait or Bahrain are available and only a few central Saudi bases, such as Al Kharj, may be used.

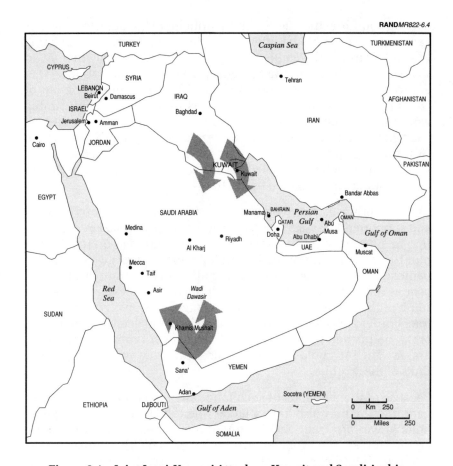

Figure 6.4—Joint Iraqi-Yemeni Attack on Kuwait and Saudi Arabia

The Potential Military Value of Israeli Assistance

Yemen is probably incapable of sustaining a major offensive into Saudi territory. However, their attack serves Iraqi purposes both by tying down Saudi forces and putting additional strain on basing options. In particular, the air base at Khamis Mushait, home of the F-117 force in Desert Storm, is very near the Yemeni border.

One option for achieving the three principal U.S. objectives in this campaign—stopping the offensive, building up forces, and evicting the enemy from all occupied territory—would be to rely mainly on GCC forces to deal with the Yemeni attacks while concentrating U.S. efforts on stemming the Iraqi attack. GCC forces operating out of Oman, the UAE, and any usable bases in southern Saudi Arabia would attack Yemeni forces, interdict their logistics, and destroy what elements of the Yemeni air force manage to get airborne. These GCC forces could be augmented by some U.S. assets, such as B-52s, which would be less suitable for early operations against the more capable air defenses fielded by the Iraqis.

As in the previous two scenarios, U.S. forces operating out of Israel and supported by assets in Egypt would range out 1000 km or so into Iraq in support of those forces that can be stationed on the limited number of available bases in Saudi Arabia and elsewhere on the peninsula. Given the need to bring all available combat power to bear against advancing Iraqi forces, it might be necessary to employ some of these forces on even longer-range missions into the Saudi-Iraqi border area. Supporting such attacks could demand that tanker orbits be pushed into contested airspace over northwestern Saudi Arabia. The IAF could help secure air supremacy over that area with CAPs of these orbits.

Because of the demands of such long-range operations, in this scenario the IAF may also have a larger role to play in offensive operations in western Iraq. As U.S. forces focus their attacks on enemy ground forces, IAF units could supplement coalition forces in, for example, interdiction attacks and counter-Scud missions. Again, prepositioning would be highly desirable to rapidly achieve high sortie rates.

IRAQ AND YEMEN ATTACK SAUDI ARABIA, ACCOMPANIED BY IRANIAN OPPORTUNISM

Scenario Description

This scenario is essentially the same as the above "Iraqi-Yemeni attack" scenario, with the added complication of possible Iranian intervention. Like the regimes in Baghdad and Sana', the clerical regime in Iran faces a deteriorating economy and declining public support. For most of the 1990s, inflation had run an average of over 60 percent a year, and unemployment had hovered around 30 percent. Disgruntlement with the regime is widespread; each month seems to witness yet another riot over prices or official corruption. Efforts to consolidate the position of Supreme Leader Khamenei have succeeded on the surface—he is not criticized by any major figure in Iran—but they have unmasked the regime's shallow ideological basis. Nonregime religious figures no longer support the regime, and corruption in the government is widespread. In 1996 and 1997, Tehran, Tabriz, and Mashad experienced riots that were put down with extreme force.

The regime itself is in a bind. It cannot afford to continue providing the relatively generous benefits it does to poorer Iranians—the regime's core support group. Moreover, many clerical members of the government do not accept the reformers' claim that the government must cut back on social services from economic necessity. Thus, attempts to escape the fiscal mess through reform are politically impossible, leading the government to rely on its military to gain new sources of revenue.

Iran gradually rebuilt its military during the 1990s. The regime devoted a substantial portion of its budget to procurement, buying a wide variety of systems at bargain prices from both China and Russia. Angered by the incorporation of Eastern European countries into NATO, Moscow in particular has proven willing to provide Iran with sophisticated weapons as part of what Russian Foreign Minister Andrei Kozyrev declared in March 1993 was a "strategic partnership" between the two nations.

Among the items Iran purchased from Russia were large numbers of MiG-31s, MiG-29s, Su-24s, and MiG-27s. Moscow has also supplied Iran with *Tupolev*-22M supersonic long-range bombers. Iran has also acquired advanced surface-to-air systems, including SA-10s and SA-13s, and may have purchased early-warning radar and electronic countermeasures. In its buildup, the regime has placed special emphasis on missiles, mines, power projection, and submarines. To this end, it has acquired large inventories of C-801 and *Silkworm* anti-ship missiles. Moreover, it has coastal artillery deployed in Abu Musa, the greater and lesser Tunb Islands, and other sites along the coast. Iran is able to produce free-floating mines domestically and has acquired Chinese missile-equipped patrol boats and anti-ship missiles that can threaten shipping in the Strait of Hormuz. Tehran now has a total of three *Kilo*-class diesel submarines purchased from Russia and five mini-submarines.

As the combined Iraqi and Yemeni attack unfolds, Iranian naval, air, and land forces mass on their side of the Gulf. The Iranian move does not appear to have been coordinated in advance with those of Iraq and Yemen. Iran evinces no indications of preparing for an attack until the Iraqis and Yemenis are well under way, and Tehran has not issued statements in support of either of these countries. The clerical regime, however, appears to have decided that the chaos in the Gulf offers an easy opportunity to expand. Iran's submarines deploy—presumably just outside the Strait of Hormuz—and anti-ship missile batteries are activated both along the Iranian coastline and on islands in the Gulf. Tehran warns that a U.S. deployment to the region will force it to close the Strait of Hormuz. Imagery indicates that mines are being loaded onto small boats in several Iranian ports.

Iranian Su-27s violate UAE and Bahraini airspace, precipitating several dogfights and causing losses on both sides. Amphibious landing units are mustering near Bandar Abbas, and Western intelligence deems an attack on the UAE and/or Bahrain as "imminent." Imagery suggests that Iran is preparing an air-defense envelope near the Strait of Hormuz. U.S. Naval forces in the Persian Gulf prepare for the prospect of fighting their way back out into the Indian Ocean (see Figure 6.5).

CENTCOM Tasking

The U.S. National Command Authority orders USCENTCOM to

- secure the necessary bases for conducting defensive and offensive operations on the Arabian peninsula

- halt the Iraqi and Yemeni offensives before key objectives—including oil facilities and important political targets—can be occupied

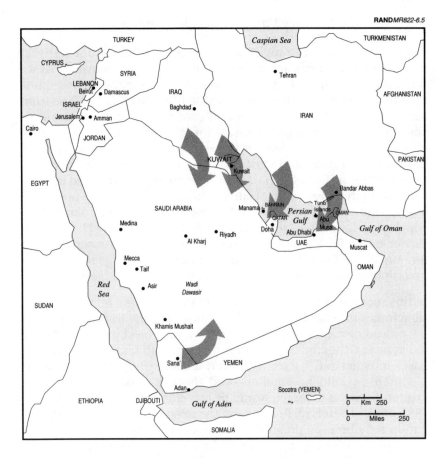

Figure 6.5—Iraqi-Yemeni-Iranian Attack on GCC

- defeat any Iranian attack on the UAE and/or Bahrain before aggressor forces can secure a foothold on the peninsula

- expel enemy forces from all occupied territory and comprehensively defeat them.

Because of the threat from the multiple prongs of the combined offensive, only a handful of bases in the northwestern part of Saudi Arabia, such as Taif, are available.

The Potential Military Value of Israeli Assistance

In many ways, this is a nightmare scenario: a three-front war that potentially could deny access to the entire Arabian peninsula. As we noted in the Chapter Five discussion of the geographic constraints on a force based in Israel, there may be little that can be done from there to support operations in and around the Strait of Hormuz. Given this fact, it may be necessary for U.S. Naval forces in the Gulf either to defend themselves until they can be relieved by task groups that force Hormuz or to fight their way out. Long-range bombers operating from Diego Garcia, Cairo West, or elsewhere could provide some support if they could negotiate the air-defense threat presented by the Iranians. One option might be a coordinated operation in which ship-launched Tomahawk land-attack missiles (TLAMs) and carrier-based EA-6 and F/A-18 aircraft provide defense suppression for, and Naval F-14s fly escort to, bombers delivering large loads of precision-guided munitions (PGMs) against Iranian targets.

In this scenario, the USAF would need to deploy the maximum possible forces into Israel (and Turkey) to combat the Iraqi attack (as in the preceding case, the Yemeni incursion may need to be handled by indigenous GCC land and air forces). Even with maximum access to bases in Israel and Turkey, however, the size of the land-based deployments would be smaller—and those forces, because of the greater distances to target, would be less effective—than they were in 1990–1991. Therefore, in this case, the need for direct Israeli participation may be even greater than it was in the preceding scenario. Some prepositioning in Israel may be a virtual prerequisite for successful U.S. air operations under these very stressful circumstances.

IRANIAN ADVENTURISM

Scenario Description

Iran's economy remains in a shambles. Oil production from Iraq and the former Soviet Union has returned to its former levels, keeping the price of oil low. Left with a deteriorating economy and declining public support, the regime decides to use its reinvigorated military to seize assets from the wealthy Gulf states or at least force them to increase the price of oil.

Tensions come to a head after widespread riots in Iran, with hundreds dying when the regime violently suppresses the rioters. Western firms, fearing instability, withdraw their investments, and Iranian merchants send as much capital abroad as possible, putting the economy into a tailspin. The regime blames the troubles on foreign agitation and notes that Gulf leaders have joined in a U.S. and Zionist campaign to keep the government crippled by overproducing oil and lowering its price. The regime calls for a production cutback from all the GCC states, as well as immediate financial "compensation" for past damage suffered. Specifically singled out for attack are the United Arab Emirates and Qatar.

The Gulf states react with alarm but do not present a united front. Within the UAE, the leadership is panicked. Dubayy, exercising its veto in federation affairs, refuses to allow U.S. forces into the country and urges the Gulf states to consider Iran's requests. In Qatar, the leadership is more unified and, while publicly urging restraint, privately has urgently requested a strong U.S. troop deployment. The GCC foreign ministers are meeting to discuss the crisis. Although they have issued a harsh criticism of Iran, they have not produced a document calling for the United States to enter the region.

Meanwhile, Iranian naval, air, and land forces are massing on the other side of the Gulf. Iran's *Kilo* submarines leave their base and deploy outside the Strait of Hormuz. Several Iranian Su-27s have violated UAE and Qatar's airspace. Intelligence reports that *Silkworm* missiles have been deployed on Abu Musa, and Iran warns that a U.S. deployment to the region will lead it to close the Strait of Hormuz.

Iran is conducting a variety of offshore operations that have the potential to threaten Gulf security. Iran's Swedish-built *Boghammar* boats are being loaded with mines, according to satellite imagery. Other Iranian surface combatants are harassing Gulf commercial traffic, particularly from the UAE, demanding to see permits and inspecting ships for contraband.

Oil experts warn that a price increase only requires creating instability or shutting down UAE production—actual conquest is not necessary. Already, speculation on the price of oil has caused a 30 percent increase in the spot price (the short-term oil market) (see Figure 6.6).

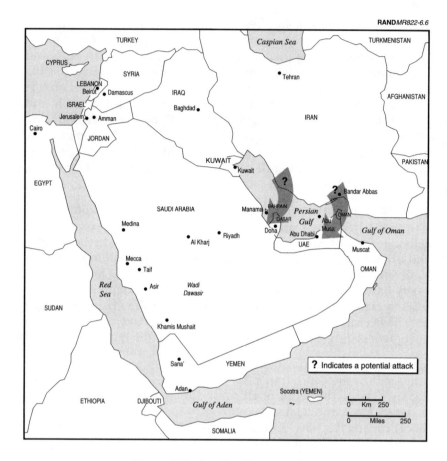

Figure 6.6—Iranian Opportunism

CENTCOM Tasking

The U.S. National Command Authority decides to deploy forces to the Gulf region to

- deter and/or defeat intervention by Iran
- prevent Iranian infiltration of Dubayy and the other emirates

- secure the flow of oil in the region, including preventing Iranian efforts to interdict tanker traffic or damage offshore oil platforms

- reassure allies in the region of the U.S. commitment to their security.

Because of Dubayy's sensitivity, no USAF units can be based on UAE territory. Basing is available in Kuwait, Oman, Qatar, and Saudi Arabia on the Arabian peninsula, and in Egypt and Israel.

The Potential Military Value of Israeli Assistance

This scenario is one in which Israeli participation would appear to be minimal. USAF access to all GCC countries except for the UAE means that adequate basing should be available for its forces without needing to operate out of Israel. As noted earlier in this chapter, Israeli bases are not well-situated for use against Iranian targets, so Israeli forces will be of little use in power projection.[7] Access to Israeli airspace could be of some use to provide a second channel of flow into Arabia.

INTERNAL INSTABILITY IN SAUDI ARABIA

Scenario Description

Both liberalizers and Islamists in the Kingdom are increasingly putting pressure on the Al Saud to reform. The reformers demand increased government accountability and citizen participation in decisionmaking. The Islamists, for their part, call for reforming Saudi society in line with conservative religious precepts. The Al Saud themselves, caught in the midst of a change in leaders after Fahd dies, are torn about which way to go. The already-low price of oil continues to fall as production from Iraq and the former Soviet Union gradually increases to its former level, limiting the royal family's ability to buy off dissent. Perhaps most important, the Al Saud no longer enjoy the same influence over the population. Oil rev-

---

[7]This may also mean that in this scenario, Israel may need coalition—and U.S.—help defending itself against possible Iranian missile attacks. Alternatively, with its right to self-defense recognized, Israel could establish both a declaratory and an operational deterrent posture versus Iran, based on its force of *Jericho* missiles.

enues have not kept up with Saudi Arabia's burgeoning population. Moreover, most of the Saudi population does not remember the days before oil wealth and thus does not consider the Al Saud to be legitimate simply for bringing prosperity to the Kingdom. Perceptions of corruption and profligacy in the Al Saud, particularly when coupled with the regime's calls for sacrifice, further embitter the Saudi population.

Tensions come to a head when Islamist figures and leaders of reformist groups call for protests of official corruption. Security forces ruthlessly suppress the demonstrations, and the regime executes several ringleaders. On the day of the executions, reformers and Islamist leaders call for Saudis to take to the streets in protest. The regime calls on National Guard units, made up of highly religious Saudi tribesmen, to restore order. After the National Guard units in Riyadh and Jeddah refuse to fire on demonstrators, the royal family flees. Riots in Mecca turn into bloodbaths, with hundreds killed in clashes between demonstrators and security troops. Occurring concurrently with the riots are sabotage attacks against industrial targets, including oil-pumping stations. Islamist groups claim responsibility and threaten to paralyze the country unless their demands are met.

Several members of the royal family who remain behind are quickly arrested, and their trials and executions are broadcast nationally. The militants set up a Revolutionary Islamic Council (RIC), which announces that it is temporarily suspending all oil shipments abroad, freezing foreign investment in Saudi Arabia, and considering cashing in many of the nation's overseas holdings and investments. World financial and commodity markets panic.

Across the country, loyal National Guard units clash with armed Islamic cells. Few regular army units are willing to take up arms against their countrymen, and some—including at least three armor battalions and several air force squadrons—declare their allegiance to the RIC. Many units simply dissolve, however, although the members often sell or give their weapons to RIC forces. Scattered fighting breaks out between turncoat Saudi units and National Guard forces.

From Cairo, Crown Prince Abdallah calls for international assistance to restore order to Saudi Arabia. To prevent such assistance, the RIC orders its forces to occupy as many oil facilities as possible and to prepare to sabotage them if foreign troops attempt to occupy the country. U.S. intelligence reports that several facilities appear to be prepared for destruction. The RIC declares its willingness and ability to launch a worldwide campaign of terror against any power attempting to intervene. The RIC also claims to have gained control of the country's CSS-2 intermediate-range ballistic missiles (IRBMs) and threatens to use them against Israel if the United States becomes involved. Several rebel Saudi F-5s rocket and strafe National Guard units in Riyadh and elsewhere. At least one exchange of fire between rebel and loyalist Saudi naval units is also reported.

Meanwhile, several of Saudi Arabia's neighbors appear to be moving to take advantage of the situation. Yemen, seeking to establish its claim to territory disputed with Saudi Arabia, sends troops north. Both Iran and Iraq mobilize their forces, but their intentions are not clear. Tehran declares that the instability in Saudi Arabia is an issue for the states and peoples of the Persian Gulf to decide.

In the United States, the President has gone on record stating that he will not allow Saudi Arabia to become another Iran. The President also echoes former President Ronald Reagan's willingness to defend the Kingdom against internal as well as external forces threatening to cut off oil supplies to the West (see Figure 6.7).

CENTCOM Tasking

The U.S. National Command Authority decides to deploy forces in the Gulf region to

- deter or defeat intervention by Iraq or Iran

- provide support to loyalist Saudi forces in their attempts to defeat organized resistance

- secure the flow of oil out of Saudi Arabia

- secure or neutralize the Saudi IRBM force.

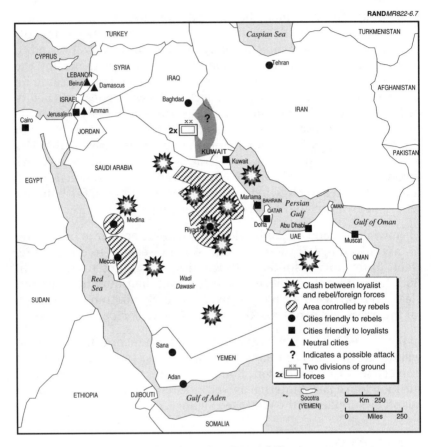

RAND*MR822-6.7*

Figure 6.7—Saudi Instability

Because of the internal chaos in Saudi Arabia, no USAF units can be based in its territory. Basing is available in Kuwait, Oman, the UAE, Qatar, and Bahrain on the Arabian peninsula, and in Egypt and Israel. Stocks prepositioned in Saudi Arabia are not available and are assumed likely to fall into rebel hands.

The Potential Military Value of Israeli Assistance

This scenario is really two in one. So long as the situation remains that of supporting the Saudi regime against an indigenous insurgency, it should be possible to base adequate forces on the periphery of the peninsula. Israeli bases are usefully close to areas in northern Saudi Arabia, and some assets could be deployed there. There appears, however, to be little direct role for the IAF in this scenario. Should the situation explode into a full-scale conflict with either Iran, Iraq, or both, Israeli bases and forces could play a similar role to that described in the scenario of the joint Iraqi-Yemeni attack above.

Using Israel as a base from which to launch operations in support of Saudi loyalists might result in serious political problems. Such a move would make potential allies in the Arab world uneasy, particularly if they feared internal unrest in their own countries. Moreover, the militants might use any Israeli support to the Saudi loyalists to discredit those loyalists, further reducing the level of domestic support for the Al Saud.

INTERNAL DISORDER IN IRAQ AND IRANIAN ADVENTURISM

Scenario Description

Sanctions and the resulting economic dislocations erode support among the Sunni elite for Saddam Hussein, whose regime is already despised by both the Kurds in the Northeast and the Shi'a in the south (see Appendix A). Leading Sunni tribes chafe under Saddam's rule and grow increasingly restive, while he responds by relying increasingly on individuals from his home area of Tikrit. Finally, a coup led by disgruntled tribesmen in the military and intelligence services topples Saddam. However, the coup splits the Sunni core of the regime into pro- and anti-Tikriti factions, and the Shiites in the south rise up. A separate southern entity will both weaken Iraq as a counterweight to Iran and raise the potential for another Iranian client in the region.

All Iraq's neighbors are alarmed by the events. Kuwait and Saudi Arabia renew efforts to woo and buy Shiite leaders in the south, but religious differences prove divisive. The GCC foreign ministers meet and issue a statement recognizing the new government of Iraq and appealing for unity. Turkey, meanwhile, is alarmed at the Kurdish gains and consolidation in the north, and is sending troops toward the border. Jordan and Egypt call for an end to the fighting and urge all outside powers to promote reconciliation rather than warfare.

Iran, meanwhile, is rushing troops to the northern Kurdish border to ensure that its own large Kurdish population does not get restive. In the south, it claims to be providing only humanitarian assistance. However, Friday prayer leaders have called for the faithful to help their brethren in the south, and Iranian officials have noted that many soldiers have "volunteered" to go fight in the south. Satellite imagery detects several Iranian divisions moving toward the Iraqi border, and Iranian aircraft are being deployed to bases in southwestern Iran. Iranian hovercraft and *Hengam*- and *Hormuz*-class amphibious assault ships also are deploying in the region, possibly as part of an operation to occupy Warba Island and the Fao Peninsula. Tehran has also publicly called for states of the region to settle problems by themselves, explicitly warning the GCC states that "Gulf populations will rise up and resist attempts to bring the forces of arrogance into the region."

Concerned about the implications of an Iraqi collapse and Iranian encroachment, the United States requests access to several bases in Saudi Arabia, Bahrain, and Kuwait. Manama refuses to grant the United States increased access, fearing Iranian subversion against the regime. The UAE also refuses to grant the United States access, although leaders from Abu Dhabi privately inform U.S. officials that Jebal Ali can serve as an emergency facility in the event of hostilities. Meanwhile, U.S. intelligence is receiving sporadic reports that Iran has deployed air-defense units, including advanced surface-to-air missiles (SAMs) and mobile command, control, and communications (C3) systems, into southern Iraq.

CENTCOM Tasking

The U.S. National Command Authority decides to deploy forces to the Gulf region to

• deter any overt Iranian move into Iraq.

On the peninsula, basing is available in Saudi Arabia, Qatar, Kuwait, and Oman. Forces can also be deployed into Egypt and Israel (see Figure 6.8).

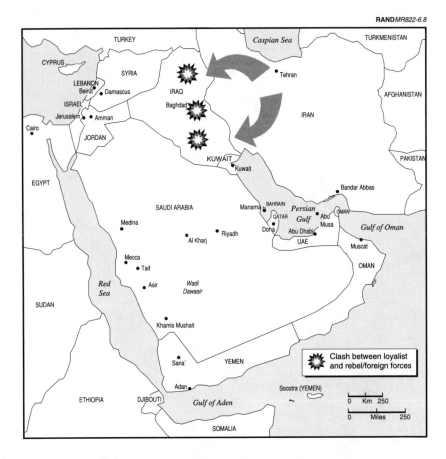

Figure 6.8—Iraqi Collapse and Iranian Opportunism

The Potential Military Value of Israeli Assistance

Both geography and the availability of basing in Saudi Arabia make Israel a marginal player in this scenario. Ranges to the Iran-Iraq border area are roughly comparable for bases in either central Saudi Arabia or Israel, which could allow Israel to serve as at least a partial substitute should access to Saudi installations be denied or restricted.

Chapter Seven

IMPLICATIONS FOR GULF SECURITY AND THE U.S. AIR FORCE[1]

In this chapter, we present our conclusions on the effects a possible Arab-Israeli peace could have on U.S. security policy toward the Persian Gulf region and recommend steps that can be taken to encourage cooperation between Israel and the Gulf countries. If peace progresses, the United States will face fewer complications in defending the Gulf in the future. Israel itself might even come to play a role over time. For this possibility to be realized, however, the United States will have to work with both Israel and the Gulf states and encourage them to become security partners.

IMPLICATIONS FOR GULF SECURITY

Peace between Israel and the Arabs will enhance the United States' ability to protect its interests in the Persian Gulf. A comprehensive peace should help gain access to the region if a crisis occurs, ease frictions arising from arms transfers, and permit streamlining of the U.S. military command structure. Peace will also decrease the pressures on Gulf leaders and their sensitivities to a U.S. presence in the region.

The chief effect of peace in the near term will be indirect. With peace, the interruptions and uncertainties that have plagued Gulf–U.S. cooperation in the past should diminish. No longer will the

---

[1]Because this report focuses on the needs of the U.S. Air Force, it does not explore the implications of peace in as great detail for the other Service branches. Of course, the implications of peace for all the Services deserve careful and comprehensive treatment.

Arab-Israeli dispute threaten existing cooperation or act as a barrier to expanded ties. Although pressure from Islamic militants and other opponents of a greater U.S. presence is not likely to diminish, at least one bone of contention will be gone. Furthermore, other states outside the Gulf will be freer to cooperate with the United States. Egypt, for example, might be more willing to host U.S. forces were the Palestinian issue resolved, and Syria might be less likely to oppose the Gulf states' cooperation with Washington.

If a crisis similar to Desert Storm occurred in the future, Israel could probably be an accepted, but passive, member of the coalition. Although peace will not eliminate the political advantages accruing to a state that attacks Israel as Saddam Hussein did in 1991, it will reduce them, especially if the Arabs will accept that Israel has the right to defend itself if attacked. U.S. forces probably could conduct military missions from Israeli and, possibly, Jordanian territory without drawing Gulf criticism.

Prepositioning equipment in the region and logistics in general will be easier to accomplish in a peace. Increased prepositioning in Israel for Gulf contingencies would be an option more acceptable to the Arabs after peace. Israel, however, would be likely to see prepositioning as a dual-use arrangement whereby U.S. supplies act as a war reserve for Israel as well. Israel can provide overflight to the Gulf to complement the Egyptian corridor.

Over time, Israel is likely to become less sensitive to arms sales to the Gulf. After peace with Egypt, Israeli opposition to arms sales to Cairo lessened, but Israel still sought to keep its qualitative edge. Israeli opposition to sales to smaller Gulf states will probably be the first to diminish, because these sheikhdoms and emirates would pose little or no possible threat to Israeli security in the event of a regime change.

POTENTIAL ISRAELI CONTRIBUTIONS

If peace progressed to the point that a direct Israeli role in the Gulf was possible, Israeli forces could contribute significantly to Gulf security. As the scenarios in Chapter Six make clear, Israel can play an important, if at times limited, role in helping the United States ensure the security of the Persian Gulf. Here, we briefly recapitulate the main conclusions to be derived from the sections on the potential military value of Israel. From them we can derive the potential security advantages to be gained from an Arab-Israeli peace:

- Part of any true Arab-Israeli peace must be mutual recognition of all parties' right to self-defense. This in and of itself could make a major contribution to Gulf security by neutralizing the kind of coalition-splitting tactics Saddam attempted in 1991.

- Access to Israeli airspace and bases could be valuable in sustaining an air bridge to the Gulf. In particular, access to Israeli and Jordanian air space would be vital if Egypt should deny or severely restrict overflight in a future contingency. Similarly, if Turkey should deny the United States the use of its facilities, the value of Israel's contribution would increase.

- The contribution of Israel would be magnified if ties improve between Israel and Jordan. The right to traverse Jordanian airspace would make Israel a more valuable transit point and improve Israel's ability to engage in active self-defense measures. Without access to or control over Jordanian airspace, operations out of Israel to points eastward would be impractical.

- Indirect Israeli participation in Gulf security—intelligence-sharing, arms sales, provision of spare parts, technology transfers—could both enhance the GCC countries' self-defense capabilities and further cement relations between the Arabs and Israelis.

- For the most part, the value of basing in Israel is *directly* proportional to the size of the conflict and *inversely* proportional to the amount of access available on the Arabian peninsula. Specifically, if Saudi bases are not usable by the USAF, Israel can provide at least a partial substitute for most scenarios involving conflict with Iraq.

- Israel and Turkey together offer a valuable combination of bases and assistance, including substantial ramp space and access to a wide variety of potential targets in the Gulf.

- The main role of the Israeli Defense Forces in general, and the IAF in particular, will be to protect Israel itself and thereby free coalition assets to prosecute the main campaign.

- Although it is somewhat limited by doctrine, equipment, training, and geography, the IAF could make a direct contribution to some stressful Gulf contingencies both by freeing up USAF aircraft to perform other tasks (by patrolling CAP orbits to protect tanker and AWACS operations, for example) and by undertaking such offensive operations as lie within its capability range (e.g., interdiction in western and southwestern Iraq).

U.S. STEPS TO ENCOURAGE GULF-ISRAEL COOPERATION

The above benefits of peace will not occur without U.S. leadership. Dialogue, pressure, and institutional changes all are necessary to encourage cooperation.

A first U.S. step must be to convince both Israel and the Gulf states that they should work together. The U.S. negotiating position with Israel is strong. With the end of the Cold War, many advocates of tighter budgets are questioning the tremendous U.S. aid to Israel. Therefore, Israel has an incentive to demonstrate its security value to skeptics. Moreover, many possible elements of the peace process may depend on U.S. support—such as the use of U.S. troops to monitor an agreement over the Golan Heights. Thus, Israel has an incentive to agree to U.S. requests for access to Israeli facilities and assistance during a Gulf crisis. The Gulf states, for their part, need to recognize that their neighbors are highly aggressive and that Israel could play a constructive role in ensuring their security.

The United States should consider encouraging cooperation among GCC states, Israel, the United States, Turkey, Jordan, and Egypt on Gulf security. It might start such cooperation by facilitating political and military dialogue among these states. Given the sensitivity of issues involved, the political dialogue would have to occur at the highest levels. Interaction among military forces should encourage habits of cooperation and foster exchange of ideas on regional security and how to deal with threats to regional order.

The United States should also encourage confidence-building measures to allay mutual suspicions. Supplying communication links to support dialogue during crises, exchanging military personnel, and instituting other measures to prevent misunderstandings should be encouraged.

Institutional changes also will help foster cooperation. The existing multilateral working groups, such as the arms-control group, should be expanded into other issue areas. These groups not only provide a forum for cooperation on issues of mutual concern, they also facilitate direct contacts between Israeli and Gulf personnel, reducing mutual suspicions.

Changing the Area of Responsibility for CENTCOM to include Israel, Syria, and Lebanon, which are currently under EUCOM responsibility, also might facilitate U.S. efforts to encourage regional cooperation. A common AOR will facilitate U.S. planning efforts, allowing planners to take advantage of any synergies that might occur from including Israeli facilities and forces in Gulf scenarios. Perhaps more important, a common AOR will lead to improved personal ties among U.S. military personnel, Israeli officials, and Gulf leaders. Such ties will improve cooperation in the event of a crisis. Exercises, staff visits, and other exchanges between Israel and the Gulf Arab states would likely be greatly facilitated if one command had responsibilities governing the entire region.

Incorporating former belligerents into the same AOR is not unprecedented. Greece and Turkey, for example, remain hostile toward each other, yet both are in EUCOM; indeed, common security interests toward other powers may have ameliorated their conflict somewhat.

The role of Turkey in the region and in the military command structure also needs to be reexamined. Like Israel, Turkey has considerable military capabilities and is concerned about Iran's and Iraq's intentions in the region. Thus, Turkey should be incorporated into planning for crises in the region. During the Cold War, when the focus of Western militaries was the Soviet Union, placing Turkey within EUCOM was sound. Today, however, facilities and forces in Turkey are likely to be called on when a crisis occurs in the Middle East, as they were during Operations Desert Storm and Provide Comfort. Thus, dual-hatting Turkey or otherwise arranging for both CENTCOM and EUCOM to have authority there is worth exploring.

FUTURE FAULT LINES

THREE FAULT LINES

The abatement of the Israeli-Arab conflict reduces the salience of one of the traditional fault lines in the Middle East. The end of the Cold War reduces another. What, then, are the likely fault lines that will most influence Middle Eastern politics in the future? The likely issues are threefold:

- fundamentalist versus nonfundamentalist Islam

- ethnic disputes

- the remnants of Arab nationalism.

All these potential fault lines will not be active at the same time, but the actual configuration may involve overlapping conflicts that produce surprising alliances of convenience.

Fundamentalist Versus Nonfundamentalist

Currently, a major source of conflict in many Middle Eastern countries is a dispute between anti-Western religious militants and their governments. Algeria is engulfed in a civil war between religious militants and military forces. In Egypt, radical Muslim groups have attacked Coptic Christians and Western tourists, as well as regime officials. Syrian President Hafez al-Assad has successfully repressed the fundamentalist movement in his country, but it could resurface if the Assad regime weakens or collapses. Even in conservative Saudi

Arabia, religious groups are critical of the regime and have at times taken up arms against the monarchy. The vast majority of fundamentalist strength and support comes from indigenous groups, but outside powers such as Sudan or Iran could help train and arm militants, increasing their ability to fight a secular regime.

Such outside support for domestic militant groups could turn religious militancy into a regional fault line. Already Egypt has been highly critical of Iran and Sudan, claiming that both are behind radical groups in Egypt. Since one of the driving forces behind political Islam is anti-Westernism, the fundamentalist movement could overlap with radical Arab nationalists and others who seek to undermine the West's influence in the region.

Over time, disputes are likely to develop within the fundamentalist camp. As with other monolithic ideologies, Islamic fundamentalist governments are likely to profess their allegiance to a common principle but, in reality, quarrel bitterly over who will be the leader of the faithful and which doctrine is the correct one. Such divisions are especially likely between Sunni militant regimes and the Islamic Republic of Iran, whose Shiite doctrine is anathema to many devout Sunnis. Although such disputes will weaken the fundamentalist camp, they may prove yet another source of instability for the already-turbulent Middle East.

In the event of a division between fundamentalists and non-fundamentalists, closer ties to Israel could be problematic for secular Arab regimes. A positive attitude toward Israel would open the regime up to powerful propaganda attacks. However, it could provide the regime with important military and intelligence benefits. Except in such specialized areas as agriculture or medicine, Israeli economic assistance probably would not be a major factor in forming regime attitudes. Were the threat high (as it was in Jordan in 1970), however, almost any regime would consider turning to Israel to stay in power, particularly if it could do so quietly or indirectly.

Ethnic Differences

Although, in general, ethnic groups in the Middle East do not currently appear poised for communal strife, the potential for conflict along these lines remains. In the past, ethnic differences were a major force in the region's longest war, that between Iran and Iraq, and another Persian-Arab dispute could emerge in the future. Moreover, the Kurds remain a nation without a state and are found in four area countries: Turkey, Iraq, Iran, and Syria. The breakup of the Soviet Union raised the potential that Azeris in Iran would seek greater ties to the new state of Azerbaijan, a possibility initially encouraged by Baku.

If ethnic fault lines should open, the non-Arab states would have an incentive to seek closer relations with Israel, given that their likely opponents would be Arabs. An interesting alliance of convenience would group Turkey and Israel against Syria if the current Israeli-Syrian negotiations fail to result in a peace agreement or if a subsequent Syrian government abrogated the treaty. Turkey and Syria themselves are currently in a low-level dispute over water rights, a divide that could grow over time as resource constraints become more pressing on both countries.

In any case, the United States might be caught between friendly non-Arab states and Arab allies such as Saudi Arabia.

Arab Nationalism

Although the defeat of Saddam Hussein appears to be yet another nail in the coffin of Arab nationalism, we cannot rule out the possibility that another ambitious leader will seize on this theme to justify aggression. Such a leader might try to use anti-Westernism as a justification, given that anti-Western sentiment remains strong in the Middle East. A nationalist leader might criticize the West for abetting divisions within the Arab world while calling for unity in resisting further Western interference. As with Islamic militancy, the opponents of a nationalist leader would be of two minds about cooperating with Israel.

POTENTIAL CHANGES IN THE REGION

In trying to understand future fault lines, we must speculate about the strength of current ideological trends in the region—something very difficult to do. However, these ideological trends have a tremendous influence on the region's geopolitical alignments. A decline in the attractiveness of Islamic fundamentalism would be the greatest determinant of change, particularly if the Iranian regime collapsed and the subsequent leadership rejected Islam as a basis for regional participation. It would greatly accelerate the integration of Israel into the region.

"Arab socialism," as practiced in Egypt and Algeria, has been discredited by the economic stagnation and corruption in these countries. For the Arab world to turn to market economics (as Latin America did after economic stagnation during the 1980s) could dampen anti-Western sentiment and thus make it easier for Israel to be integrated into the region.

Finally, Arab perceptions of Israel could change. This is unlikely. But given that half of Israel's population is made up of immigrants from the Arab world or their children, it will be increasingly difficult to sustain the myth of Israel as an inherently alien power in the region.

Another potential change could occur in the outside powers that influence the region. The United States is currently the predominant power, but both Russia and China have commercial interests in the Middle East and are eager to sell the region arms. Russia also has interests in Turkey, Iraq, and Iran, given their proximity to Central Asia, which Moscow claims as a sphere of influence. Beijing is becoming increasingly dependent on oil from the Gulf region, and may also have political motives in building ties to the Middle East; such ties could serve as a way to relieve or counter U.S. pressure on China. Even ostensible allies such as France see the United States as an economic rival in the region. Any of these countries could try to limit cooperation between Arabs and Israel and exploit tension by criticizing U.S. ties to Israel.

THE STATE OF U.S.–ISRAEL COOPERATION TODAY

The close relations between the United States and Israel stem from shared cultural bonds, U.S.–Israel strategic ties, and the well-organized pro-Israel sentiment in the United States. U.S.–Israel security cooperation is extensive but often informal. The United States has frequently aided in Israel's defense, but Washington does not have the formal commitment to do so as it does with the NATO nations. Several executive agreements, however, commit the United States to meeting Israel's security needs (Safran, 1978). Military cooperation includes joint planning, combined exercises, and intelligence-sharing (Bill and Springborg, 1990).

In addition to Israel's strategic value as a reliable friend in an unstable and important region, many Americans also support Israel for religious or other ideological reasons. Many observers consider the pro-Israel lobby to be one of the most powerful and effective lobbies in the United States (Tivnan, 1987). A large proportion of America's 6 million Jews support Israel staunchly, and many non-Jews in the United States, particularly fundamentalist Christians, support U.S. aid to Israel (Bill and Springborg, 1990).

Israel is particularly important for the U.S. Navy. Roughly half of all Eastern Mediterranean port visits of the U.S. Sixth Fleet are in Haifa, and many U.S. ships use the repair and servicing facilities there. Roughly 50,000 sailors and Marines take shore leave in Israel each year.

The United States and Israel also cooperate closely in many defense industries. Israel is the United States' largest partner in the ballistic-missile-defense arena. Israel is part of such programs as the *Arrow* anti-tactical ballistic missile system and the anti-cruise missile *Nautilus* system. The U.S. military tests and procures Israeli defense systems, including *Pioneer* unmanned aerial vehicles (UAVs), Single-Channel Ground and Airborne Radio System (SINCGARS) radios, and the HAVE-NAP long-range air-to-ground missile.

The United States also plays an important role in Israel's economy. As much as 7 percent of Israel's tourist revenues in 1993 was generated by U.S. military visits, and the United States is Israel's largest trading partner. Moreover, the United States annually provides Israel with roughly $3 billion in assistance—the largest amount given to any foreign country.

The United States aids Israel with its diplomacy as well as its armed forces and aid dollars. Israel has long relied on the U.S. veto in the United Nations Security Council to counter anti-Israel resolutions from member states. However, with the end of the Cold War and progress on peace, such anti-Israel sentiment has diminished in the United Nations, as suggested by that body's recent repeal of the "Zionism is racism" resolution.

U.S. diplomacy has played a crucial part in Israel's efforts to make peace with its Arab neighbors and with its own Palestinian population. The United States helped broker the initial Israeli–Egyptian disengagement after the 1973 War and then led the parties to a formal peace, enshrined in the 1979 Camp David Accords. After the Persian Gulf War, the United States was a major force in getting peace talks going between Israel, the Palestinians, and Israel's neighbors.

ON WEAPONS OF MASS DESTRUCTION

Looming over any possible large contingency in the Persian Gulf is the specter of nuclear, biological, or chemical (NBC) warfare. Recent revelations about the extent of Iraq's pre-war biological-warfare program and chronic concern over the state and future of Iranian nuclear research highlight the importance of this issue.

Given the context and scope of this study, we were led to wonder whether the changing political landscape of the region could alter the role NBC weapons might play in U.S. Air Force (USAF) operations. In particular, would access to Israeli bases be of any value is defusing the NBC threat from an adversary?

To answer this question, we plot range rings indicating distances 500, 1000, and 2000 km from Baghdad (Figure C.1). The principal NBC threat in the Gulf region would likely emerge in the form of warheads delivered on medium-range and intermediate-range ballistic missiles (MRBMs and IRBMs).[1] The figure shows that any Iraqi missile system with a range of about 1000 km could hit targets anywhere in Israel and across northern Saudi Arabia.[2] Missile launches from further south in Iraq would have a greater footprint in Saudi Arabia

---

[1]On a tactical level, artillery is an important means of delivering chemical weapons but is clearly beyond the scope of this analysis. Aircraft can, of course, deliver NBC weapons of all varieties. Our belief, however, is that U.S. air defenses will remain sufficiently strong to make air attacks on the friendly rear area a very high-risk, low-payoff option for any Gulf adversary.

[2]As a point of reference, the Iraqi *Al Abbas* Scud variant has an estimated range of 900 km. The *Al Aabed* IRBM, reportedly under development by Iraq in the late 1980s, is estimated to have a 2000-km range. North Korea has been developing a family of

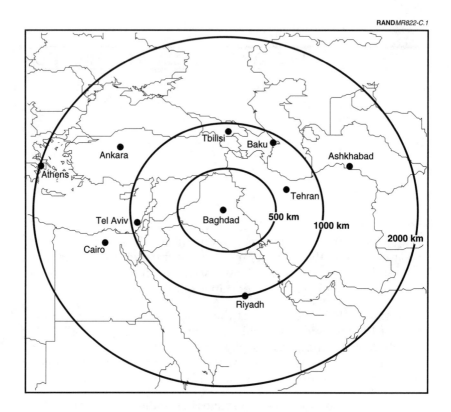

Figure C.1—Missile-Range Rings from Iraq

while still covering all of Israel. Geographically, then, Israeli bases offer no advantage over Saudi ones in the face of a missile threat from Iraq.

One benefit Israeli basing might offer is a preexisting ballistic-missile-defense capability. Deployment of the U.S.–Israeli *Arrow* missile-intercept system would provide some level of protection for USAF assets deployed at Israeli facilities. While Saudi Arabia is procuring some number of *Patriot* missile batteries, a requirement to

---

MRBM/IRBM systems with ranges between 1000 and 3500 km. India's *Agni* "technology demonstrator" has a 2500-km range. Data are from D.S. Lennox, ed., *Jane's Strategic Weapon Systems*, London: Jane's, 1990.

deploy additional units into the theater will likely remain if point defense is needed at numerous air bases. Such deployments take time and consume airlift resources that could otherwise be used for additional air or ground combat forces—especially important in the early days of a contingency.

To answer the same question for Iran, in Figures C.2, C.3, and C.4 we show missile-range rings from three points in Iran: one near Tehran, and one each in the southeastern and southwestern parts of the country. From the Tehran site, a missile with a range in excess of 1500 km would be required to cover most of Israel and Saudi Arabia below Riyadh; the 1000-km circle does, however, cover most of Saudi

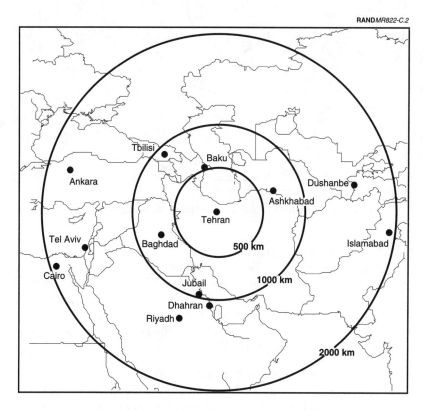

RAND*MR822-C.2*

Figure C.2—Missile-Range Rings from Tehran

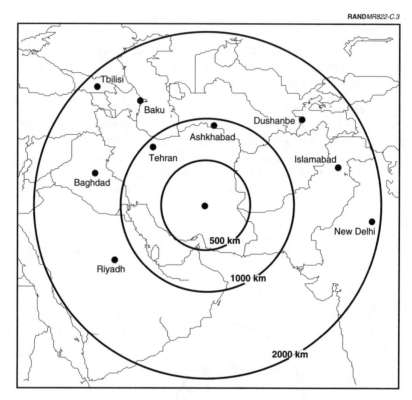

Figure C.3—Missile-Range Rings from Southeastern Iran

Arabia's northeastern province, the site of many valuable oil-producing-and-processing facilities and brings ports and air bases in the Jubail/Dhahran area into range. Launching from the south-eastern site would bring all of Saudi Arabia's Gulf coast within the 1000-km circle, at the cost of putting Israel outside even the 2000-km ring and, perhaps more important from Tehran's perspective, putting Baghdad 1500 km away.

Launched from southwestern Iran, a missile with a range of 1000 km could strike points throughout Iraq and in most of Saudi Arabia from Riyadh north. Israel would be out of reach of launchers with ranges of 1500 km or less from locations in this area.

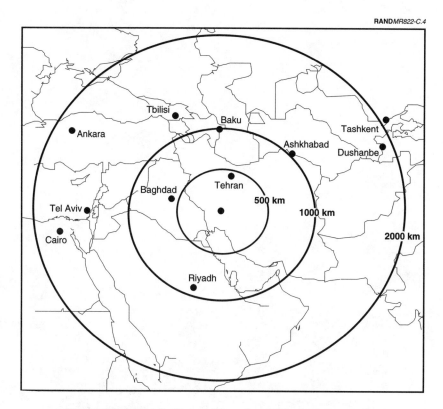

Figure C.4—Missile-Range Rings from Southwestern Iran

These simple geographic facts seem to accord perfectly with our findings regarding the relative utility of Israeli bases in conflicts with Iran and Iraq. Just as distance makes Israeli facilities less useful in a confrontation with Tehran, it renders them safer from attacks originating in Iran. Whether the advantages offered by any in-place Israeli ballistic-missile defense would offset the increased vulnerability of its bases to Iraqi attack will, of course, depend in great measure on the extent and capabilities of those defenses, as well as on the specifics of the contingency.

BIBLIOGRAPHY

Amos, John W., and Ralph H. Magnus, "Regional Perceptions of the American Central Command," *Conflict*, Vol. 5, No. 4, 1985.

Bill, James A., and Robert Springborg, *Politics in the Middle East*, New York: HarperCollins Publishers, 1990.

Binder, Leonard, "United States Policy in the Middle East: Toward a Pax Saudiana," *Current History*, January 1982.

Buchan, Glenn C., and David Frelinger, *Providing an Effective Bomber Force for the Future*, Santa Monica, Calif.: RAND, CT-119, 1994.

Carter, Jimmy, "The State of the Union," in *Weekly Compilation of Presidential Documents*, Vol. 16, January 28, 1980 (Speech delivered on January 23, 1980).

Cordesman, Anthony, *The Gulf and the Search for Strategic Stability*, Boulder, Colo.: Westview Press, 1984.

———, *The Gulf and the West: Strategic Relations and Military Realities*, Boulder, Colo.: Westview Press, 1988.

———, "The Saudi Arms Sale: The True Risk, Benefits, and Costs," *Middle East Insight*, Nos. 4/5, 1986.

"Deal by Enron with Qatar," *New York Times*, January 20, 1995, p. D16.

Frelinger, David, Joel S. Kvitky, Gary Liberson, and Charles Neerdaels, *Bomber Flexibility Study: A Progress Report*, Santa Monica, Calif.: RAND, DB-109-AF, 1994.

Gordon, Michael R., and Bernard E. Trainor, *The Generals' War: The Inside Story of the Conflict in the Gulf*, Boston: Little, Brown and Company, 1995.

"Israeli Prime Minister Sees Sultan in Oman," *New York Times*, December 30, 1994, p. A2.

Johnson, Maxwell O., *The Military As an Instrument of U.S. Policy in Southwest Asia: The Rapid Deployment Joint Task Force, 1979–1982*, Epping, England: Bowker, 1984.

Keaney, Thomas A., and Eliot Cohen, *Gulf War Air Power Survey (GWAPS) Summary Report*, Washington, D.C.: U.S. Government Printing Office, 1993.

Kechichian, Joseph A., *Political Dynamics and Security in the Arabian Peninsula Through the 1990s*, Santa Monica, Calif.: RAND, MR-167-AF/A, 1993.

Kheli, Shirin Tahir, and William Staudenmaier, "The Saudi-Pakistani Military Relationship," *Orbis*, Spring 1982.

Kupchan, Charles A., *The Persian Gulf and the West: The Dilemmas of Security*, Boston: Allen and Unwin, 1987.

Lennox, D. S., ed., *Jane's Strategic Weapon Systems*, London: Jane's, 1990.

McNaugher, Thomas L., *Arms and Oil*, Washington, D.C.: The Brookings Institution, 1985.

———, "Balancing Soviet Power in the Persian Gulf," *Brookings Review*, Summer 1983.

Newsom, David, "America Engulfed," *Foreign Policy*, No. 43, Summer 1981.

Peters, Joel, *Building Bridges: The Arab-Israeli Multilateral Talks*, London: The Royal Institute of International Affairs, 1994.

Pindyck, Robert S., and Julio J. Rotemberg, "Energy Shocks and the Macroeconomy," in Alvin L. Alm and Robert J. Weiner, eds., *Oil Shock: Policy Responses and Implementation*, Cambridge: Ballinger Publishing Company, 1984.

Quandt, William, *Decade of Decisions: American Policy Toward the Arab-Israeli Conflict, 1967–1976*, Berkeley: University of California Press, 1977.

———, "Riyadh Between the Superpowers," *Foreign Policy*, No. 44, Fall 1981a.

———, *Saudi Arabia in the 1980s: Foreign Policy, Security, and Oil*, Washington, D.C.: The Brookings Institution, 1981b.

Ross, Dennis, "Considering Soviet Threats to the Persian Gulf," *International Security*, Vol. 6, No. 2, 1981b.

Rowen, Henry S., "U.S. Vulnerability to an Interruption in Gulf Oil Supplies," in Edward R. Fried and Nanette M. Blandin, eds., *Oil and America's Security*, Washington, D.C.: The Brookings Institution, 1988.

Safran, Nadav, *Israel: The Embattled Ally*, Cambridge: Harvard University Press, 1978.

Sicherman, Harvey, "The United States and Israel: A Strategic Divide?" *Orbis*, Summer 1980.

Spiegel, Stephen, "Israel as a Strategic Asset," *Commentary*, Vol. 75, No. 6, 1983.

Sterner, Michael, "The Gulf Cooperation Council and Persian Gulf Security," in *Gulf Security and the Iran-Iraq War*, Washington, D.C.: National Defense University Press, 1985.

Stork, Joe, and Martha Wenger, "From Rapid Deployment to Massive Deployment," in Micah L. Sifry and Christopher Cerf, eds., *The Gulf War Reader*, New York: Times Books, 1991b.

Tivnan, Edward, *The Lobby: Jewish Political Power and American Foreign Policy*, New York: Simon and Schuster, 1987.

U.S. Department of Defense, *Conduct of the Persian Gulf War: Final Report to Congress*, Washington, D.C., 1992.

Wohlstetter, Albert, "Half Wars and Half Policies in the Persian Gulf," in W. Scott Thompson, ed., *National Security in the 1980s: From Weakness to Strength*, New Brunswick: Transaction Books, 1980.

Yorke, Valerie, "Security in the Gulf: A Strategy of Pre-emption," *World Today*, July 1980.